GEOLOGY OF OUR
WESTERN NATIONAL
PARKS AND MONUMENTS

GEOLOGY OF OUR
WESTERN NATIONAL
PARKS AND MONUMENTS

Royle C. Rowe

Binford & Mort

Thomas Binford, Publisher

2536 S.E. Eleventh • Portland, Oregon 97202

Dedicated with love to my sister,

LORRAINE L. ROWE

and with appreciation to the officials of

THE NATIONAL PARK SERVICE

GEOLOGY OF OUR WESTERN

NATIONAL PARKS AND MONUMENTS

Copyright © 1974 by Binfords &
Mort, Publishers. Printed in the
United States of America. All rights
reserved. No part of this book may
be reproduced in any form without
written permission of the publishers.
ISBN: 0-8323-0237-6
Library of Congress Catalog Card
Number 73-13278
Second Edition 1977

FOREWORD

Freeman Tilden, noted conservationist and author of "The National Parks - What They Mean to You and Me," has said that "the chief aim of interpretation is not instruction, but provocation." Tilden would be the last to maintain that a publication like this one - "Geology of Our Western National Parks and Monuments" - should contain all provocation and no instruction. What he would expect, I believe, is that certain quality of instruction and knowledge which makes the material attractive and understandable.

The reader of this book senses that the author has tried hard, with significant success, to achieve the goal of interpretation so succinctly defined by Tilden. He distills key geological facts and concepts about each of the western national parks and monuments in the geological category from the immense mass of available literature. He is both instructive and provocative in conveying to the reader the variety, magnitude and majesty of the geological forces and processes which have shaped the scenic and scientific wonders of our western parks and monuments. The author probably raises many more questions than he answers. However, I am sure he would be greatly pleased if his readers thirst for further knowledge and are stimulated to satisfy their curiosity by reading, visiting these national park and monument wonderlands, or by any other means.

ROBERT H. ROSE
Chief Geologist (Retired)
National Park Service

PREFACE

Possibly half a million visitors were coming annually to our national parks at the time when the National Park Service was created as a bureau of the Department of the Interior in 1916. For 1968, one news release reported ". . .a record high of 150,835,600. . ."

The NPS report, "Public Use of the National Park System," shows these annually increasing visitations:

1970: 165,538,000
1971: 192,059,400
1972: 202,237,900

Approximately 33 million of these were made in 1972 to the 52 areas of the 13 Western States discussed here. The service is introducing new regulations limiting numbers of campers and the length of their stay, and is considering even barring automobiles from some over-crowded seasonal areas, substituting instead bus service within park boundaries, plus construction of exterior parking sites and interior multi-lane highways.

Yet among these millions who arrive eagerly each year to admire and photograph the colorful grandeurs, far too many depart with only an incomplete comprehension of the major geologic backgrounds involved.

The primary purpose of this booklet is therefore that of attempting a semi-scientific compilation of such principles, compromising between a brief pamphlet and a more detailed and expensive text. Many excellent descriptions of National Park Service areas already have been published, but these sometimes do minimize geology by the inclusion of much history, biology, camping information, highway material, or personal comment. Other beautifully emphasize the photographic aspect but offer too little geologic explanation for the origin of scenes portrayed. Finally, some of the books recently published are scientifically detailed and colorfully illustrated but rather expensive for the average reader.

Many national monuments as well as most of the seashores and memorials require little geologic comment. In contrast, there are several areas of unique geologic origin, although not under NPS supervision, which are herein discussed and illustrated. Finally, for various reasons, the writer is including only the thirteen most westerly states containing the majority of national parks and monuments of geologic nature.

Acknowledged references, as well as many others, together with National Park Service bulletins, have been freely consulted with regard to factual data. Personal correspondence with park officials who checked respective pages of this manuscript has added to the accuracy and modernization of this revision.

A large number of the photographs are reproduced from the files of the NPS Bureau of Visual Information; others are from black-and-white or color views taken by the writer or from other sources authorized as stated, particularly Ward's Natural Science Establishment, Rochester, N.Y., or Mac's Foto Service and Stewart's Photo Shop, both of Anchorage, Alaska.

No maps of National Park or Monument areas are provided in this volume, on the assumption that the visitor will have obtained such from among the free brochures at the N.P.S. information desks. Highway maps and library references are also good informational sources.

ORIGIN OF THE
NATIONAL PARK SYSTEM

Yellowstone is the first and largest of our National Parks. It is located mainly in northwestern Wyoming, but extends also into Montana and Idaho a few miles. Its discovery and development have been detailed in so many references that a brief summary will suffice here.

The famous Lewis and Clark Expedition assembled at the Falls of the Ohio River near Louisville, Kentucky in 1803, spent the winter in preparation, and started out from St. Louis, Missouri in 1804. After crossing the Rocky Mountains under the guidance of the Indian woman, Sacajawea, they wintered along the Pacific coast, then temporarily divided into two parties for separate explorations of the Marias and Yellowstone Rivers, then returned to St. Louis in the fall of 1806.

John Colter, a former soldier with the expedition was the first known white man to reach the Yellowstone Park area . In 1807, after assisting the Manuel Lisa group in setting up a fort at the mouth of the Bighorn River, a tributary of the Yellowstone, he was given the solitary task of further exploration and also encouragement of Indian trading. Reaching the Jackson Hole country via the Bighorn and the Shoshone Rivers and Wind River Mountains, he returned along the shore of Yellowstone Lake, crossed Mount Washburn, reached the Grand Canyon of the Yellowstone, fording the river near Tower Falls. He failed to arrive at the famous geyser basins, but saw smaller geysers near the lake. He described the thermal activity of the area so vividly when he came back three years later that for long thereafter the region was dubbed "Colter's Hell."

By the 1830's, many scouts and trappers, including Jim Bridger, were relating exaggerated tales of the wonders of the area.

In 1869 a party of three spent a month or more exploring the Yellowstone region. Their report led to the Washburn-Langford-Doane Expedition of 1870. This group included General Henry D. Washburn, then Surveyor-General of the

Montana Territory, Nathaniel P. Langford, a vigilante officer who later became the first superintendent of Yellowstone Park, and Judge Cornelius Hedges of Helena, Montana. The party left Helena on August 17, and at Fort Ellis it was joined by Second Lieutenant Doane and a squad from the U.S. Army 2nd Cavalry.

Following almost four weeks of investigation, they were camped homeward bound near the junction of the Madison, Gibbon, and Firehole Rivers on September 19. Discussion brought up the suggestion by Judge Hedges that a National Park be created for public pleasure and the idea was enthusiastically accepted.

Dr. F.V. Hayden, veteran geologist of several National Surveys, headed a scientific party into the Yellowstone area in 1871. This group, including the famed pioneer photographer, William Henry Jackson, and the renowned artist, Thomas Moran, made scientific studies and obtained a photographic and art record of the area's wonders. The work of these three men gave impetus to the bill to establish Yellowstone National Park, which was enacted by Congress, and signed by President Ulysses S. Grant on March 1, 1872.

The arch at the Gardiner, Montana entrance, for which the cornerstone was laid by President Theodore Roosevelt in 1907, bears the inscribed keynote of the National Park System: "For the Benefit and Enjoyment of the People." A photograph of this arch, reproduced from a color slide taken by the writer years ago, is shown on the next page.

The National Park Service was created by Congress in 1916 during the administration of President Woodrow Wilson. Franklin K. Lane was Secretary of the Interior at that time, and Stephen T. Mather was the first appointed Director, with 11 parks and 18 monuments under his supervision. At present (1972 data) a total of 38 National Parks have been designated, plus more than 290 assorted Monuments, Seashores, also Historic Sites, Memorials, Recreation Areas, and Parkways.

Entrance arch at Gardiner, Montana — dedicated by President Theodore Roosevelt in 1907. Its inscription reads:

"FOR THE BENEFIT AND ENJOYMENT OF THE PEOPLE"

(From color slide by the writer)

OBJECTIVES AND POLICIES OF THE NATIONAL PARK SYSTEM

A National Park Service brochure of July 10, 1964, entitled "A Road to the Future," contains an introduction by Stewart L. Udall, Secretary of the Interior, in which he refers to the establishment of the Service by the Congressional Act of August 25, 1916, and a letter from Franklin K. Lane, then Secretary of the Interior, to Stephen T. Mather, the first Director. Udall mentions this letter as being sometimes called the Magna Carta of the National Parks.

The brochure mentions the three general categories of areas within the System and defines them as follows:

1. Natural areas — the great scenic wonderlands. . .

2. Historical areas — examples of the ancient Indian cultures, as well as buildings, sites, and objects. . . of American history.

3. Recreational areas — providing the healthful outdoor recreational opportunities for a population . . .increasingly urban.

Among the detailed criteria for natural areas are included:

1. Outstanding geological formations or features significantly illustrating geologic processes.

2. Significant fossil evidence of the development of life on earth. . .

10. Examples of the scenic grandeur of our natural heritage.

CONTENTS

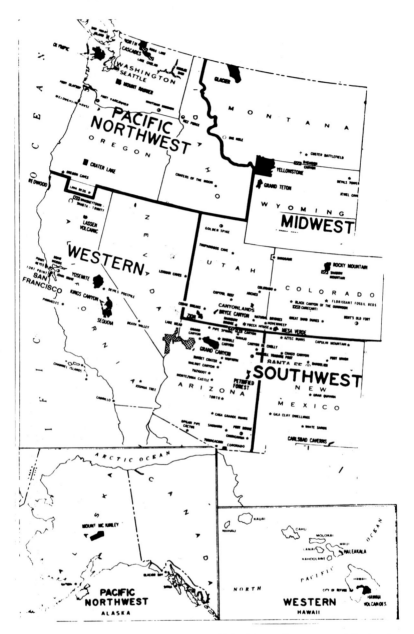

United States Department of the Interior

NATIONAL PARK SYSTEM
Western Regional Groups, States, and Areas

4

*Year of authorization, regardless of boundary
or name changes.

5

GEOLOGY OF OUR
WESTERN NATIONAL
PARKS AND MONUMENTS

Million
years
ago

GRAPH: Scale of 100,000,000 years = 1 inch.

Million years ago	Epochs	Periods	Eras
2	Pleistocene	Quaternary	
12	Pliocene		
25	Miocene		
40	Oligocene		
55	Eocene		
65	Paleocene	Tertiary	Cenozoic
135		Cretaceous	
180		Jurassic	
225		Triassic	Mesozoic
275		Permian	
325		Pennsylvanian	
350		Mississippian	
400		Devonian	
425		Silurian	
500		Ordovician	
600		Cambrian	Paleozoic
4,600	Line extended 40 in. farther down.		Precambrian

GEOLOGIC TIME

Mother Earth constantly insists that she is much older than we have thought. The geologic time table undergoes constant revision, particularly as extending the duration of the oldest division, the Precambrian. The current estimate of the total age of the earth since attaining present size is at least 4.6 billion years, although the oldest exposures of rocks are estimated by radioactivity calculations at about 3.5 billion years; moon samples of rock have been estimated to be of similar age.

Such an immense time duration is incomprehensible in comparison with human life and history. For instance, if one compares these 4,600,000,000 years to an average lifetime of 75 years, then each million years will correspond to slightly less than 6 days!

Geologic time is divided primarily into eras, which in turn are subdivided into periods and epochs, just as years are proportioned into months and days.

Eras:	Periods:	Epochs:	Duration: (in millions of years.)	Time since:
Cenozoic	Quaternary	Recent		
		Pleistocene	2	2
"Age of	Tertiary	Pliocene	10	12
Mammals"		Miocene	13	25
		Oligocene	15	40
		Eocene	15	55
		Paleocene	10	65
Mesozoic	Cretaceous		70	135
"Age of	Jurassic		45	180
Reptiles"	Triassic		45	225
Paleozoic	Permian		50	275
"Age of	Pensylvanian ⎫ Carbon-		50	325
Inverte-	Mississippian ⎭ iferous		25	350
brates"	Devonian		50	400
	Silurian		25	425
	Ordovician		75	500
	Cambrian		100	600
Precambrian or Azoic or Cryptozoic			4,000	4,600
"Age of Primitive Life or None"				

Central front of John Hopkins Glacier, with visitors' cruise boat in the foreground.   (National Park Service)

A L A S K A

GLACIER BAY National Monument (Glaciation)

Glacier Bay National Monument, within southeastern Alaska, is officially stated as being unequalled in the National Park System in exemplifying glacial activity in phases both of advance and retreat, history of tide water glaciers, and the interaction between glaciation and life forms. Recession of Muir Glacier alone exposes 1,600 to 1,800 feet of new land each year, showing ice age cyclic action.

The monument has a total area of 4400 square miles, beginning about 100 miles northwest of Juneau. Glacier Bay is 70 miles long, with about 20 very large glaciers, many small ones, 10 fjord-type inlets, and many floating icebergs.

Because snow and ice accumulation in this region is so rapid, many of the glaciers push downward to the coast, terminating in high ice cliffs which may break off, forming icebergs, or may hang inert at the mouth of the valley.

The action of wind and waves may often force the drifting of icebergs up onto the beaches along the coast line, where melting then produces fantastic shapes.

Glaciation

Muir Glacier is one of the most active Alaskan glaciers, and its remarkable retreat has been studied extensively since 1890. It is almost 2 miles wide, with an ice face rising about 200 feet above the bay. Its rate of accumulation and advance is extremely rapid, from 20 to 30 feet per day, whereas most glaciers only move an inch or two per day, with a foot or so considered fast. The balance between the upper accumulation of snow and ice and the lower melting rate under increased warmth of the sun at less elevation regulates the position of the ice front, which in the case of Muir Glacier results in its rapid rate of retreat.

A sheet of ice up to 4,000 feet thick covered all the bay as recently as in the year 1700, but retreated thereafter. An earthquake in 1899 shook the ice floes, destroying frontal portions of Muir Glacier, and choking the bay with icebergs to such an extent that tourist boat trips to the ice cliffs were cancelled. Following this event, recession was rapid, and by the year 1913 Muir Glacier had moved its terminal face back 8 miles. Another 15 mile retreat was accomplished by 1970, leaving a cabin which John Muir had built at the tip of the glacier in 1890 now 23 miles from the terminus.

Terminus of Muir Glacier with icebergs in Glacier Bay, which lies between the St. Elias Range to the east and the Fairweather Range westward. (From color slide by Mac's Foto Service)

Glacier Bay occupies a valley between two parallel, lofty mountain ranges, higher than any within the contiguous United States. On the east is the ice-capped St. Elias Range, dominated by 18,000-foot Mount St. Elias 140 miles northwest in Canada. This range feeds Muir, Cushing, Rendu, and related glaciers. Cushing and Rendu Glaciers are blocked by moraines, and no longer reach the sea.

On the west is the Fairweather Range, with Mount Fairweather, 15,320 feet high, on the northwest boundary. Some of the glaciers originating in this range are Johns Hopkins, Brady, Reid, Grillon, and Lituya, the last one melting into Lituya Bay. The Hugh Miller and Guincy Adams Glaciers no longer reach the sea, being likewise obstructed by their moraines.

12

The position of the terminus of any glacier, as previously stated, is due to the net balance between replenishment of snow and ice high on the slopes and melting in lowland areas, with deposition of moraines at front and sides. Rapid advances of the ice in the area may also be due to elevation of the Fairweather Range and nearby mountains, plus their proximity to the moist winds off the Gulf of Alaska, as well as the constrictive shape of Glacier Bay. The 70-mile recession of Muir Glacier on the east side of the bay contrasts with the current 3-mile advance of Brady Glacier on the west.

The century-long periodic fluctuations of glacial movement are indicated by the layers of vegetal growth. As retreat occurs, the barren, rocky ground and weathered tree stumps are uncovered, then overgrown by fungi, lichens, and mosses.

Mountain avens, i.e. small multi-colored flowering plants of the rose family, are even more vital for stabilizing and reconditioning the post-glacial soil later on. They are also accompanied by fireweeds, horsetails, dwarf willows, and alders. After many years of fertilization from plant growth and decay, hemlock and spruce forests again cover the area, only to be destroyed once more by the next cycle of glacial sand and gravel deposition during flood conditions, plus erosion during the next advancement of the ice.

Glacier Bay thus has become noted as a major area for all aspects of glacial study.

KATMAI National Monument (Volcanism)

Near the northern part of the Alaskan Peninsula and across Shelikof Strait from Kodiak Island is Mount Katmai, famed for its 1912 eruption and for the associated Valley of Ten Thousand Smokes. Both areas, as well as most other volcanic peaks nearby, are now almost inactive, although Mount Trident has produced a few small lava flows quite often since 1953 and other adjacent peaks show fumaroles. A mile-wide lake now occupies Katmai's crater and another exists in Kaguyak Volcanic Crater.

Katmai National Monument, including an area of more than 4,200 square miles, was created in 1918, two years after the National Geographic Society Expedition led by Dr. Robert F. Griggs had discovered the area. Later it was extended to include the Naknek Lake game area.

Interestingly enough, for 45 years or more Mount Katmai was blamed solely for the eruption, even in recent geology texts. Later studies by the U.S. Geological Survey, however, have revealed the true site of explosive action as having been Novarupta Volcano, six miles westward, although Katmai was beyond doubt a part of the cataclysm.

Geologic History

The bedrock formations of the valley are not volcanic, but fossiliferous sandstones and shales of Jurassic age, lying nearly horizontally, and overlain in some places by lavas from older volcanoes such as Mageik, Knife Peak and Trident. Katmai was once a cone-shaped peak like the others, until the eruption of 1912.

In early June of that year the peaceful valley was subjected to a series of vigorous earthquakes, causing rock slides from Falling Mountain. Fissures opened in the valley floor, from which incandescent pumice and ash was spewed out, flowing as much as 15 miles distant before hardening. Some of this was hot enough to weld itself together as a tuff, underlying the later actual lava flows from the craters. Smoke and steam must have issued from many places in the valley, although no eye-witnesses were at hand.

A terrific explosive blast of steam and other gases, pumice, rock fragments, and hot ash burst from Novarupta

14

Volcano during the morning of June 6, with others at frequent intervals. An estimated 2½ cubic miles of ash shot into the atmosphere, covering about 40 square miles of the valley to depths of many feet. The first major explosion of Mount Katmai occurred that afternoon, and more or less simultaneously, the craters of Martin, Mageik and Trident responded.

The major explosion was heard as far as 750 miles away at Juneau, and also northward across the Alaska Range at Dawson and Fairbanks. Dust formed a haze in the atmosphere, reddening sunsets over more than half of the northern hemisphere, and continued to fall for three days afterward.

Kodiak, almost 100 miles away across Shelikof Strait, was darkened and covered with 6 to 12 inches of ash.

The summit of Mount Katmai completely disappeared, leaving only a stump-like rim surrounding a huge caldera about 3 miles long and 2 miles wide. For this reason, scientists long believed that Katmai had literally disintegrated itself.

Air view of Mount Katmai Crater after the eruption of June 6, 1912.
(National Park Service)

Dr. Robert F. Griggs, after his visit to the site, analyzed three theories regarding this conjecture in the National Geographic Society volume, "The Valley of Ten Thousand Smokes."

First, he states that such a quantity of material would have provided a layer 16 feet in depth extending 10 miles in every direction.

Second, the formerly quiet magma beneath Katmai perhaps made its way through subsurface passages into the main conduit of Novarupta, where it exploded outward and upward. Underlying support thus being removed, Katmai may have largely collapsed into its own crater.

Third, the older magmatic material beneath Katmai was a dark, andesitic batholith which accumulated much gas as it stoped its way upward and toward Novarupta. The newer volcanic material which erupted was a white, acidic rhyolite, bearing fragments of the darker material in its own mass. So apparently the old mountain was partially melted into the new magma, as an addition to other factors.

A native of a village twenty miles north of the volcano is reported to have given a short visual account of the eruption to Dr. Grigg's group. He stated that the villagers used boats to travel down Iliuk Arm of Naknek Lake to the village of Naknek, during the darkness caused by falling ash. Almost unbelievably, no lives were lost!

The first visitors to the valley in 1916-1917 saw thousands of the fumaroles in action, spouting superheated steam with such force that a frying pan had to be held downward against the vent pressure. The 1919 National Geographic Society Expedition found these greatly diminished in both numbers and temperatures. By 1950 less than 100 were active, and at the present time less than a dozen remain.

Yet in curious contrast to all this thermal turmoil, one tiny L-shaped glacier 10 miles long flows down the northwest crater wall of Mount Katmai toward Mount Griggs, and deep, steep-sided canyons have been eroded in the tuff of the valley floor.

MOUNT McKINLEY National Park (Glaciation, Biology)

Mount McKinley is well known as the highest peak in North America, towering in a spectacular fashion about 18,000 feet above its basal plateau and the McKinley River to reach a summit elevation of 20,320 feet on its higher South Peak.

Located near the southwestern climax of the Alaska Range, which sweeps across the south-central part of Alaska as a 600-mile arc lessening in elevation as it joins with the Coast Range north of the St. Elias Mountains, midway between Anchorage and Fairbanks, it is approximately 250 miles south of the Arctic Circle.

The peak itself is quite inaccessible to the average visitor, although excellent views are seen from along the highway between Park Headquarters and Camp Denali, 88.5 miles to the westward.

Seen across Wonder Lake, 85 miles from the entrance, Mount McKinley is only 27 miles distant across the river. The Eilson Visitor Center, at Mile 65.2, also provides good views of Muldrow Glacier and various peaks.

The present automobile route branches westward from Paxson on the Richardson Highway to follow the Denali Highway to the park station 160 miles northwestward. A

Snow-covered Mount McKinley — view toward southwest from Stony Hill.   (From color slide by Mac's Foto Service)

17

new highway is recently being constructed to connect more directly with Anchorage and Fairbanks, as does the Alaskan Railroad which has a terminus at the park entrance not far from where it crosses the continental divide at its lowest elevation in North America, only 2337 feet.

Geological study of Mount McKinley began in 1902 with the efforts of Alfred H. Brooks, the first white man to ascend its slopes, and D.L. Raeburn of the U.S. Geological Survey. North Peak, while not the true summit, was first climbed in 1910 via Muldrow Glacier. In 1913 South Peak was successfully ascended by way of its north side, and in 1951 its western face was at last scaled.

Geologic History

Mount McKinley is not of volcanic origin, contrary to beliefs of many persons. It consists of a mass of granite intruded at the close of the Mesozoic Era through Paleozoic and Mesozoic sediments topped by black marine slate, now greatly metamorphosed and deformed. Structurally the peak is a synclinorium, i.e. a regional down-warping with subordinate folding. It is transversed by a large number of faults crossed by lesser ones, forming the various valleys and mountain passes. Rock types from nearly all geologic periods, plus varied igneous formations, are present.

Snow and glaciers continually cover the upper portion of the mountain, the largest being on the less accessible southern slopes where moist winds from the Pacific Ocean increase precipitation.

An excellent and popular view may be obtained from Stony Hill Overlook, about four miles east of Eilson Visitor Center on the highway. The summit of Mount McKinley is seen toward the southwest.

Muldrow Glacier on the north side is 35 miles long, being formed from Peters, Traleika, and Brooks Glaciers in a northeastern direction, then turning northward with its terminus, now stagnant and covered with rocks and vegetation, reaching to within one mile of the highway a few miles west of Eilson Visitor Center. Usually retreating, it did advance about four miles in 1956. Herron and Foraker Glaciers flow northward from Mount Foraker, whose elevation is 17,400 feet.

Ruth and Tokichitna Glaciers flow from the south face of Mount McKinley. Eldridge Glacier, descending from the southeast slope of Mount Mather, is another notable one. Yentna Glacier has a beautiful pattern of both medial and lateral moraines.

Yentna Glacier, on Mount McKinley's southern slope — famous for its beautiful lateral and medial moraines. (National Park Service)

Pleistocene glaciers produced the usual spires, arretes, U-shaped valleys, grooved and striated surfaces, moraines, outwashed plains, kettles, and erratics. The last are very large boulders often transported many miles by the ice, and differing from the local bedrock.

Because of the load of gray glacial silt carried by the many streams, these split into numerous channels separated by sandbars or islands, forming a braided pattern. The great load of sediment makes it impossible for the stream to erode laterally, and the bars at low water provide an easy method of fording the stream.

There is a definite relationship between the types of fauna and flora in the park and the three environments. Timber line falls about 3000 feet above sea level, causing three distinct life communities: the barren perennial snow fields uppermost, the Alpine tundra between 3000 and 5000 feet elevation, and the northern forest below. The tundra consists of two types: the upland dry portion, and the lowland wet area. The dry portion is better drained, so plants are stunted or dwarfed. Plants grow more densely in the wet zone, including shrubs, willows, and the dwarf birch.

Below timber line is the northern forest, where spruce, balsam poplar, aspen, and more than 400 species of wild flowers are known. The smaller forms of animal life are present, such as the porcupine, red fox, hare, and beaver. Many birds are present, some found in both the tundra and the forest, others only in one or the other.

This shows the close relationship which exists between the glacial zones and climates and the life forms of different elevations. The highway alternates between forest and tundra from the park entrance to Eilson Visitor Center, but the tundra dominates after these 65 miles.

WASHINGTON

MOUNT RAINIER National Park (Volcanism, Glaciation)

Mount Rainier is the highest peak in the Cascade Range, with an elevation of 14,410 feet — only slightly below that of Mount Whitney in California at 14,495 feet, the highest in the 48 contiguous United States. It is about 60 air miles southeast of the heart of Seattle, and almost due east of Olympia. Beautifully visible from these and adjacent cities on clear days, but often obscured by clouds or haze, it is an excellent example of the volcanic, glaciated cones of the Cascades, and what may be said of its origin applies to all other peaks of this range.

Mount Rainier — reflected in a mountain lake near its base which provides a beautiful mirrored image.   (National Park Service)

Geologically, these might equally be classed and discussed among the results of glaciation, since Mount Rainier especially is noted for its development of the largest single-peak system of glaciers in the original United States, i.e., exclusive of Alaska. Hawaii, of course, has none.

Geologic History

Hundreds of millions of years before, thousands of feet of Paleozoic and Mesozoic sediments and volcanic beds had accumulated in western Washington and the general coastal region. Therefore the Cenozoic rocks in these states rest on a basement complex of igneous, sedimentary, and metamorphic rocks, widely eroded to a coastal plain of gently rolling topography with western drainage by the Tertiary Period, about 65 million years ago.

Western Washington was thus a region of swamps and deltas, in which sand, clay and peat accumulated. As the coastal plain sank slowly, the sediments collected at a similar pace, until the 10,000 feet of the Eocene Puget Group, consisting of sandstone, shale, and coal, had been formed. Plant remains and wave-ripple marks indicate its shallow water origin.

A notable change occurred in the Oligocene Epoch, less than 40 million years ago, when submarine volcanoes rose upon the sinking coastal plain where Mount Rainier exists now, and became islands. Steam explosions from the combination of molten rock and sea water caused complete shattering of the lava into fragments which flowed over large areas of the underwater surface. This formation of breccia and sandstone, the Ohanapecosh, is likewise 10,000 feet or more in thickness.

Following the close of this submergence and volcanism, the area was again uplifted several thousand feet, with a sidewise compression of the beds into shallow folds into which deep valleys were eroded.

The great Miocene eruptions and lava flows, 20 to 30 million years ago, produced two types of volcanic rocks. The earlier were pumice flows down the slopes of more distant volcanoes which formed a welded tuff through their own heat and buried the hilly landscapes under a volcanic plain created by the Stevens Ridge formation. Later, a series of lava flows from low angle volcanoes were laid upon each other as basalts and andesites, now named as the Fifes Peak formation.

During the closing portion of the period, after these volcanoes had ceased eruption, the rocks were again compressed and uplifted into broad folds, or moved along great faults. Molten rock masses intruded the previous layers, cooling into a granodiorite resembling a granite, but containing somewhat higher proportions of dark basic minerals. This rock is well known in Mount Rainier National Park in various localities.

During the Pliocene Epoch the final topographic change occurred, perhaps between 3 and 12 million years ago, when the Cascade Range began its slow rise while rivers such as the Columbia simultaneously cut deep valleys into its peaks and ridges.

Mount Rainier undoubtedly originated several hundred thousand years ago with flows of thick lava down the slopes of its early cone, followed by the deposits of pumice and thinner flows which form the magnificent cone as now seen. Activity of the last 10,000 years also includes subsequent eruptions, reported as recently as the middle of the 19th century, such as that by Captain John Fremont in 1843, with others perhaps as late as 1894, although some authorities consider the last to have been only dust clouds from rockfalls. So it seems quite possible that Mount Rainier may erupt again at some future date, since steam and heat are known to exist in ice caves near its summit.

All of the volcanic cones of the Cascade Range, notably Baker, Glacier Peak, Rainier, Adams, and St. Helens of Washington, then Hood, Jefferson, Three Sisters, and ancient Mazama (now holding Crater Lake) of Oregon, and Shasta and Lassen of California were formed at this time and have similar histories. Lassen Peak is the only recently active one, having erupted last in 1914.

This question of dormant heat in the Cascade Range, interestingly enough, was mentioned in *The Oregonian* of May 2, 1973 with regard to Mount Hood.

The article states that Richard Bowen, an Oregon

geologist, has begun preliminary study at the mountain's fumarole area to try to discover whether heat is increasing in the dormant volcano. Some flight photographs were made of areas not covered with snow for comparison with similar ones taken several years ago at a similar time, to determine whether any larger snow-free areas may now exist.

Bowen mentions the significance of (a) the mountain being one of the explosive type, (b) its proximity to a closely populated area, and (c) its known activity only slightly more than a century ago. If his preliminary studies show any significance, he may attempt to obtain approval for infrared scanning of the region. Seismological studies of earth movements amid the dormant Cascade Range volcanoes might possibly be authorized by the Legislature, as well.

Glaciation

More glaciers occupy the steep slopes of Mount Rainier than on any other peak in the United States, with the exception of Alaska. They may vary from 50 to 500 feet thick, with a total area of 34 square miles, as heretofore stated. Like most of the world's glaciers of today, they have been receding quite rapidly except for recent, slow advances of a very few, perhaps only temporarily. Position and movement of the face of any glacier is the result of the balance between rate of accumulation of ice at the head in contrast to the rapidity of melting at the face under the influence of lower elevation and higher daily temperature.

Of the total of 41 remaining, covering about 34 square miles, 15 are classed as of major size. They originate either within huge cirques between 10,000 and 12,000 feet elevation, or at the summit Icecap itself. Most of them are "live" ones, flowing down slopes at about 16 to 20 inches daily.

Emmons Glacier, on the northeastern side, is the largest, being about 5 miles long and a mile wide. These two are probably the better known and most accessible, together with Paradise Glacier, somewhat smaller, which often will form beautiful ice caves within a 3-mile hiking distance from Paradise Inn.

Ice cave within a glacier on Mount Rainier, such as Paradise Glacier.
(National Park Service)

Nisqually Glacier, on the southeastern slope, can be seen from 11 miles away along the new Stevens Canyon road, and its upper part is visible at Paradise. A half mile walk west of the Paradise Visitor Center offers a good view of the major part of the glacier.

Continuing along the highway from Paradise to Longmire, one soon crosses the Nisqually River. During the late 1930's the writer remembers Nisqually Glacier as being only a short walk upstream from the highway, with a large ice cave near by. The snout of the glacier, about 100 feet thick, now protrudes from the left (north) side of the lower valley approximately a mile upstream. There is a trail for visitor use leading toward it, although lately park officials have been warning them against trying to approach too closely, as there is always danger from rocks sliding down the unstable slopes. The front of Nisqually Glacier recedes perhaps 70 feet per year at present, while the ice itself advances about 25 feet.

Terminus of Nisqually Glacier, which originates just below the summit and flows southward to within a mile of the Paradise Visitor Center,
(National Park Service)

NORTH CASCADES National Park (Glaciation, Diastrophism)

North Cascades is among our recent national park additions. It is divided into two portions, a northern and a southern, separated by the Skagit River Canyon, or Ross Lake Recreation Area, while southeasterly from the tip of the southern portion is the adjacent Lake Chelan Recreation Area. Located here are the town of Stehekin and the head of Lake Chelan, a glacial valley only a mile or so at the greatest width, yet with a depth of 8,500 feet from top to bottom -- practically down to sea level -- as one of the deepest gorges on the continent.

The Cascades extend from the Fraser River in Canada southward beyond Oregon, and are among the major mountain ranges of the world, influencing the climate and vegetation over a great part of the Pacific Northwest.

Geologic History

Prior to the close of the Mesozoic Era the whole region was uplifted and depressed many times, after which the Cenozoic lavas spread over it at successive intervals. Warping produced the Calkins Range, with a width greater than that of the Cascades which developed later. Ancient volcanoes of that time released gray andesite flows along the axis of the future Cascade Range.

The immense basaltic lava flows of the Columbia Plateau then spread over this region as well as into eastern Washington and Oregon and parts of adjacent states. Some 200,000 square miles were covered -- the largest expulsion of fissure lavas in geologic history, comparable only to the vast flows of the Dekkan Plateau of India. Uplift began after the Miocene flows had ceased and by latter Pliocene time the Cascades showed the rolling skyline similar to those of the Appalachian Range.

All these peaks were heavily glaciated during the Pleistocene Ice Age, and even today 80% of the glaciers in the 48 states occur in the park area. In the northern portion Mount Shuksan with its many glaciers rises to 9127 feet in elevation. Picket Range, studded with dagger-like spires and likewise

27

with a great many glaciers, is east of Baker River valley. The southern section is noted for Eldorado Peak, with three miles of glaciers on its sides. Many have called these peaks the American Alps.

Marblemount Entrance to the American Alps — on Washington Highway 20, east of Mt. Vernon.

New Highway Construction

For many years roads have existed from both west and east approaching the summit of the Cascade Range as Washington State Highway 20, but never crossing it. The North Cross State Highway, as formerly known, leaves its junction with Interstate 5 four miles north of Mt. Vernon, and passes eastward through Sedro Woolley, Concrete, and Marblemount, finally stopping at Newhalem. This is a "company" town headquarters for the employees of the city of Seattle at the Gorge, Diablo, and Ross dams for production of electric energy by the Skagit River.

From the east, Highway 20 left the Okanogan fruit growing area through the Methow valley via Twisp and Winthrop, ending at the alpine crossroads village of Mazama. In 1893 the Washington State Legislature appropriated $20,000 for an initial survey of a route to cross the lofty

Boulders of banded gneiss covering the Skagit River valley-bottom below Diablo Dam.

Diablo Dam, which with Gorge Dam downstream and Ross Dam above provide electrical power for the Seattle area.

peaks of the North Cascades. Construction began in 1959, and after an expenditure of $24 million and 23 years of constructional work, the 63.59-mile connecting link between Diablo Lake and Mazama was opened to the public on September 2, 1972.

The highway traveller should therefore realize that he is actually passing through the Ross Lake National Recreation Area, which separates the North and South units of North Cascades National Park, as well as portions of Baker and Okanogan National Forests. The middle 37 miles of the road will usually be blocked by snow from late October to mid-April.

After crossing Thunder Arm of Diablo Lake, the new road follows upwards along Ruby and Granite creeks to Rainy Pass at 4855 feet elevation from which can be seen a signpost marking the Pacific Crest National Scenic Trail

Rainy Pass (Elev. 4855 feet) — southward view toward Frisco Mountain and Lyall Glacier.

for hikers. Towering peaks of the Cascades are visible in all directions. Cutthroat Peak and Silverstar Mountain are visible toward the northeast. Another five miles of climbing, curving around Liberty Bell Mountain, brings one to Washington Pass, at 5477 feet elevation, where granite peaks rising to nearly 10,000 feet surround the area. Liberty Bell Mountain is seen west of Washington Pass Overlook, reached by the camera enthusiast by way of a quarter-mile access road and trail, while Vasilky Ridge, Silver Star Mountain, and Kangaroo Ridge extend from northeast to due east. All of these afford spectacular views of knife-edged ridges. Remember that this entire portion from the mouth of Granite Creek to Washington Pass and onward toward Mazama is located in the Mount Baker-Wenatchee-Okanogan National Forest areas, rather than actually in North Cascades National Park.

Silverstar Mountain, shown by (←), Vasilky Ridge toward left, and Kangaroo Ridge toward right — view westward from Washington Pass overlook.

Silver Lake and Mount Redoubt are in the far northern portion of the park area, west of Ross Lake. This aerial view from 12,000 feet shows typical glaciated scenery. There are more than 300 glaciers in the area, and the water in lakes above the dams has an apple-green color because of the "rock flour" carried into them from the gneiss and granite of the eroded peaks.

Picket   Range, southern portion, in North Unit of the National Park.
(National Park Service)

Mount Shuksan (Elev. 9127 feet) — highest within the North Cascades
National Park, far toward the northwest portion.   (National Park Service)

Silver Lake, of glacial origin — Mount Redoubt in distance. Aerial view from 12,000 feet altitude. Both are in the far northern portion, west of Ross Lake. (National Park Service)

The southern portion may be visited by following an unpaved road from Marblemount via the Cascade River valley to Stehekin, at the head of Lake Chelan. Cascade Pass, Trapper Lake, and Horseshoe Basin are scenes along this route.

Barton Glacier, on Forbidden Peak north of Cascade Pass, in South Unit of the National Park.   (National Park Service)

OLYMPIC National Park (Glaciation, Rain Forest)

The Olympic National Park in extreme northwestern Washington is perhaps more significantly related to the seasonal rainfall and snow than any other. As in other Pacific Coast states, some of its peaks are covered by glaciers which have produced the usual effects of knife-edged ridges and steep-walled lakes.

The primary park area includes 1400 square miles of primitive wilderness in the Olympic Mountains, plus a 50-mile strip of Pacific Ocean coast line extending northward from the mouth of the Hoh River. The Olympic Mountains are the highest of all the Coast Ranges, with Mount Olympus rising to an elevation of 7,965 feet at their maximum.

The peninsula which includes the park is bounded by water on three sides: the Pacific Ocean on the west, the Strait of Juan de Fuca (a part of Puget Sound) on the north, and the Hood Canal (also related to Puget Sound) on the east.

Geologic History

The oldest rock formation in the park is Lower Cretaceous in age, from about 135 million years ago, formed of eroded fragments now hardened into a gray sandstone and a dark slate. These were apparently formed in a sea which was not favorable to living organisms, since a few worm tubes are the only fossils found. Pillow lavas deposited under water are also interbedded with marine limestones.

The region was elevated sometime between late Cretaceous and early Tertiary time, and all sea water was drained from this part of the state. Erosion of the Paleocene and Eocene Epochs reduced the landmass practically to sea level, and the sea re-entered the area, only to have fissures open in the ocean floor from which floods of lava poured. In some of the localities lava beds are found to alternate with marine sediments in which fossil plants, fish, and invertebrates are found, continuing through the Oligocene and Miocene Epochs.

As this portion of geologic time came to an end, there

occurred a great uplift which produced the ancestral Olympics, a range extending from Puget Sound southeastward toward the Columbia Plateau. These mountains were similarly eroded, until the late Pliocene or early Pleistocene mountain building forces had raised the range to its present height.

Glaciation

Glaciation by the Canadian ice sheet which invaded the area four times, finally to withdraw about 11,000 years ago, was aided also by piedmont and mountain glaciers. One vast piedmont glacier, in its southward progress, split against the mountain range causing the one lobe to pass westward via the Strait of Juan de Fuca, while the other travelled to the southward into the Puget Sound depression to approximately the location of Olympia.

Sixty or more glaciers remain yet in the Olympic Mountains, three of them being two miles or more in length. Being near to Puget Sound and the Pacific Ocean, precipitation is abundant, and the permanent snow line exists at 6000 feet or less, thus perpetuating glaciers to a greater degree here than in other mountain ranges of the west. The annual rate of precipitation averages 100 inches or more at the coast, about 150 inches above the higher ridges to the eastward, and perhaps even 200 inches toward the summit of Mount Olympus, mostly between October and April.

The "Rain Forest"

Such conditions have also provided for a typical "rain forest" in which the vegetation is lush, and the world's largest trees of four species have been found. A Douglas fir 14'6" in diameter grows in the Queets River valley, and the largest known western hemlock, 8'7" through, is located along the east fork of the Quinault River. In the Hoh valley there is a Sitka spruce which is 16' through, and along the coast there occurs a 21' red cedar which is exceeded in size only by the gigantic California redwoods.

In addition to the numerous trees, the rain forest includes a tangled complex of various mosses, ferns, vines, and fungi. Wildflowers grow abundantly at nearly all elevations within the park, but are most colorful in the northeastern portions, as along Hurricane Ridge and on Mount Angeles.

Many species of animal life — amphibians, reptiles, birds, and mammals large and small — are also to be seen by the observer.

Trail through the Hoh Rain Forest — tangled mosses, ferns, vines, and fungi. Olympic Peninsula.   (National Park Service)

The Pacific Coast area, already mentioned, is most easily observed from the U.S. Highway 101, where it reaches the shore at Ruby Beach on the south side of the Hoh River, thence proceeding southward to Kalaloch and Queets, where it again turns inland.   Stacks, sea caves, and tilted wave-weathered formations are common beach scenes.

Finally, two thermal springs are notable, one at the Olympic Hot Springs site, the other at the Sol Duc Hot Springs area, nine miles apart in a straight line suggesting a deep fissure origin.   Surface temperature of the water is 130°F., favoring growth of colorful algae in the pools.

OREGON

CRATER LAKE National Park (Volcanism)

Crater Lake, about 50 miles north of Klamath Falls, lies in the caldera of an ancient volcanic peak geologically called Mount Mazama. Its growth was much like that of any other volcanic cone within the Cascade Range, as described for Mount Rainier.

As originally pictured by geologist J. S. Diller in 1902 and his successors, it was assumed to have been symmetrically conical, and probably similarly having an elevation of about 12,000 feet. Glaciers descended from its summit, as indicated by the serrated rim surrounding the lake, also by striated stones found between layers of lava which form its slopes.

View northward toward ancient Mount Mazama — approximate former profile as indicated by dotted line — estimated 10,000 to 12,000 feet in original elevation, like most peaks of the Cascade Range. (Based on the National Park Service plaque on Oregon Highway 62, south of Crater Lake.)

Geologic History

There were apparently three episodes in the later geological destruction of Mount Mazama, which must have been a fearsome, yet thrilling sight as witnessed by the Indian peoples of that region about 6,600 years ago. Klamath Indian legends tell of a war between two deity chiefs, Llao of the Oregon mountain, and Skell of California's Mount Shasta, a hundred miles southward. They believed that the gods stood on their home peaks during a seven-day battle marked by rocks flying through the air, flames shooting into the sky, mountains exploding, and dust darkening the air until the collapse of Llao's throne within itself.

Geological studies suggest that during the first of these phases violent eruptions threw tremendous quantities of pumice, ash, and dust over the region. The material was apparently derived from the heart of the old volcano rather than having been torn from the walls of the vent.

Second, incandescently glowing pumice was exploded even more violently in a series of avalanches when the volcano literally boiled over. These hot masses must have travelled at terrific speed down the slopes, as no deposits were made within the first 4 miles. Much of it flowed into Wheeler Creek Canyon, southeast of the rim, reached by a highway leading from Kerr's Notch. Here are the Pinnacles, eroded spires of pumice sometimes 200 feet high. They seem to be of a more resistant material formed around vents in the pumice deposits from which gases and steam were escaping, later to be carved by water erosion. Pumice Flat is an area along the southern entrance, Highway 62, and there are miscellaneous dry lake beds of pumice east of the mountain. Most of the pumice, however, is along the north entrance, Highway 138, from Pumice Point on the rim through the Pumice Desert, with some even having been wind-blown as far as British Columbia.

The final third stage came 6,600 or so years ago during the close of the Pleistocene Glacial Epoch, or soon thereafter, as shown by carbon-dating of animal remains in layers of dry pumice in nearby caves. Fissures opened in the sides of the volcano and elsewhere nearby, allowing from 15 to

17 cubic miles of rock to drain away into other parts of the Cascade Range magmatic reservoirs. Because of this withdrawal, the whole top of Mount Mazama collapsed, removing about 90% of the material to form a caldera 6 miles by 4 miles in elliptical dimensions, and perhaps 4000 feet deep. This theory is supported by the comparative absence of any such blocks of solid rock tossed over the countryside, or even on the slopes of the cone - perhaps 15% of the total at most.

However, as suggested by writer Phil F. Brogan, correspondent for *The Oregonian,* in the April 15, 1973 issue, some modifications of the originally imagined Mount Mazama may become necessary through further studies of the last decades, first suggested by Professor R. C. Sill of the University of Nevada and subsequent studies by University of Oregon geologists.

Crater Lake and Wizard Island — Devils Backbone and Llao Rock in background.

First, the modified picturization of the summit suggests a peak considerably below the 12,000-foot elevation first imagined, also that it may have been greatly asymmetrical with a gentle slope northward, and steeper southern slopes which provided higher protection for the accumulation of glacial ice. Glaciers on the northern side of the mountain appear to have been short, whereas those three which proceeded down the southern slope through Kerr and Sun Notches and the Munson Valley were much longer, flowing downward at least a mile below the rim, even though this was the sunny side of the mountain. Further, it is now believed that the volume of volcanic ejected material may have been less than previously supposed, probably 15 cubic miles at a maximum.

Minor subsequent eruptions formed secondary cones on the flat floor of the caldera. Wizard Island rises 760 feet above the water level today, with a small crater 300 feet wide and 90 feet deep. Soundings demonstrate the presence of two other similar cones which do not reach the surface of the lake. Growth rings on trees on the island show a life span of some 900 years.

The same soundings (1960) show a depth of 1932 feet from water level to crater floor. The lake surface at 6176 feet elevation is about half a mile below that of Hillman Peak (8156 feet) which is the highest point on the rim. Discovery Point is somewhat southward, on the west rim drive, both names commemorating a young prospector, John Wesley Hillman, who was searching for the "Lost Cabin Mine," climbed the western ridge on June 12, 1853, and saw the blue lake spread before him.

From the eastern rim, the visitor may hike to the summit of Mount Garfield (8060 feet) or follow a longer 2½-mile trail to the top of Mount Scott (8926 feet), the highest point in the Park.

As with most volcanic cones, intrusive dikes formed along the margins. The Devils Backbone, rising vertically up the west wall, is a good example. The Phantom Ship, to the southeast, has a pale green hull of volcanic ash and a brownish-black sail from a basaltic dike, intruded into the volcanic ash of the wall.

Blue Water

Crater Lake has always been noted for its exceedingly blue water, unequalled elsewhere in the world. Those who first reported the discovery used the name of "Deep Blue Lake," while a later party merely called it "Blue Lake." Its present name originated in 1869. Considerable wonder has always existed as to the cause of this marvelous color. It is not due to the reflection of the sky, which is less blue, nor to any mineral content of the water. Common belief explains the hue as being the result of the combined depth and purity of the water, which filters out or absorbs all other colors of the sunlight spectrum, reflecting only the blue and violet portions. But more than once, someone has driven many miles to see its beauty, only to find a dense fog cover everywhere!

Fog over Crater Lake — Mount Scott, highest point in the park, with Cloudcap along highway, in background.

Crater Lake is the second deepest in the Western Hemisphere, surpassed only by Great Slave Lake in Canada; five others in the world are still deeper. Water temperature is consistently 39°F. at 300-foot depth. Records show that the first time the lake froze solid at the surface was in 1949. Water level never varies more than 3 feet, as no outlet or inlet is known, so gain from snow and rainfall balances loss due to evaporation and seepage.

OREGON CAVES National Monument (Ground Water)

Oregon Caves, which is really only a single cave of four levels connected by complicated passages, is at an elevation of about 4000 feet in the Elijah Mountains of the Siskiyou Range, part of the Klamath Range of the southwestern part of Oregon. East of U.S. Highway 199, it is reached via Oregon Caves Highway 46, 20 miles east of Cave Junction.

Elijah Davidson, in 1874, discovered it while pursuing a bear with his dog. Its four levels were found later by Frank Nickerson of Kerby, Ore., who cleared several corridors of blocking stalactites.

In 1907 Joaquin Miller, the "Poet of the Sierras," referred to the cave in his writings as "The Marble Caves of Oregon." Like all caves, the cavern is within a marine limestone which here was later metamorphosed by mountain building pressures into a marble.

Geologic History

A mixture of marine and volcanic materials had accumulated during many million years in the late Triassic Period. The Pacific Coast uplift produced a group of layers of interbedded marble, quartzite, slate, and volcanics now known as the Applegate group. Instability of the crust followed the uplift, and the mountains were largely eroded away to a nearly flat surface almost at sea level. Much of southern Oregon then existed as a marine island. Uplifts in several stages formed a plateau known as the Klamath Peneplane, which increased the erosional power of the streams and aided by glaciation formed the Siskiyou Mountains.

As the underground water tables were lowered, channels developed along joints in the 200-million-year-old rock formations, and glacial waters added to the normal regional flow enlarged portions of these into various air filled passages and chambers, as in any cave system.

As usual, these surface waters plus added carbon dioxide CO_2 combined with the calcium carbonate $CaCO_3$ of the marble to form the more soluble calcium bicarbonate $Ca(HCO_3)_2$. This solution seeped through ceilings of rooms below, where evaporation and loss of carbon dioxide caused redeposition of lime again as calcium carbonate to form numerous stalactites, stalagmites, flowstones, rimstones, and other deposits. Rimstone is a special feature at the "Devil's Washboard," at the foot of "Paradise Lost," and along the tunnel floor called the "Atlantic Ocean." Waterfall formations hanging in sheets from the ceilings are particularly exquisite.

Detail view of massive stalagmites in Paradise Lost. Rimstone is shown at the bottom of the view. (National Park Service)

JOHN DAY FOSSIL BEDS National Monument
(Paleontology)

John Day was added to the National Park Service System on October 26, 1974, when Rep. Al Ullman's Congressional Measure, co-sponsored by Senators Bob Packwood and Mark Hatfield, was signed into law by Pres. Gerald Ford.

The area included some private lands, as well as three State Park sites: Sheep Rock unit, the Painted Hills unit, and the Clarno unit.

The region was primarily publicized by Dr. Thomas Condon, the "pastor with a rock pick," who came to Oregon Territory in 1853. After investigating the marvelous discovery of turtle shells and mammalian bones as described to him, he wrote to Dr. O. C. March, famed Yale paleontologist, on May 23, 1871, about the "fossiliferous rocks arranged in galleries, each painted in brightest hues of red, green, and white, endlessly mixed into neutral shades."

These explorations led to discoveries of hard, black bones of prehistoric turtles, horses, cats (including sabretooth types), wolves, dogs, camels, rhinoceroses, pig-like creatures called oreodons, and others.

Strata which underlie alluvium and Pleistocene lava flows and cinders are Tertiary in age:

Pliocene	— Rattlesnake formation
Miocene	— Mascall formation
	Columbia River basalt
Oligocene	— John Day formation
Eocene	— Clarno formation

Hundreds of tons of reptilian and mammalian fossils have been collected in the John Day area and shipped to many American universities. Dr. John Campbell Merriam of the University of California, with student groups, was among such paleontologists.

Fossil collecting is of course now strictly prohibited here, as in all NPS park and monument areas.

IDAHO

CRATERS OF THE MOON National Monument (Volcanism)

Would you like to examine the moon's surface without the necessity of space travel? A "reasonable facsimile thereof" can be seen by the visitor in the area of Arco, Idaho, to the north of Twin Falls and Pocatello.

Craters of the Moon National Monument consists of 83 square miles of cinder cones and black, frothy, twisted lava flows, many of them quite recent. While such areas are common in the western states, an unusual display of volcanic variations may be found here. Both the "aa" or rough scoria type, as well as the "pahoehoe" or ropy form of lava can be seen. Lava tubes, flows which resemble rivers and waterfalls, caves and volcanic bombs are all there, easily accessible to the view.

Ropy "pahoehoe" lava, characterized by its twisted bands formed by slow cooling as it flowed.   (National Park Service)

Geologic History

In general, geologists consider the volcanic activity here as being rift eruptions, that is, lava spurting out from cracks in the surface of the earth. Cones and craters are numerous in the North Crater Flow, also southeast of the highway where a view from Big Craters shows the spatter and cinder cone chain along the Great Rift. Big Cinder Butte is one of the world's largest purely basaltic cones. The Cave Area is toward the east, due to many places where the "pahoehoe" top hardened and the liquid material flowed from below, leaving tubes and caverns. Roads, self-guided nature trails, and ranger-guided tours assist the visitor in seeing and understanding it all.

National Park Service Ranger guiding party through a lava cave in Craters of the Moon National Monument.   (National Park Service)

The volcanic action of the Columbia Plateau in general began in the Miocene Epoch, perhaps 25 million years ago, but in this and similar areas it continued until a mere 1600 years ago. Indeed some of the lava flows in western states appear to have hardened within the last few months, so freshly glossy are the iridescent surfaces of blue, bronze, and purple.

The Tree Mold area contains impressions of charred trunks of living trees which became surrounded by cooling "pahoehoe" lava. The Great Owl Cavern is a lava tube 500 feet long, 40 feet high, and 50 feet wide. Oddest of all are the red and blue stalactites and stalagmites found in caves and tunnels. These of course are not of limestone, but are drippings of colorful lava from ceiling to floor which solidified in place. Boy Scout Cave has a floor of ice due to perpetual freezing of surface water retained under winter temperatures.

One especially interesting feature is the "Devil's Sewer Pipe," a 6-inch cylinder of lava, hollow in the center, lying at the very bottom of a crevasse about 4 feet below the surface. The explanation is that the tube was squeezed into the crack, the surface hardened through cooling, and the liquid center flowed on out. This structure regrettably was destroyed by rock collectors years ago.

MONTANA

GLACIER National Park (Diastrophism, Glaciation)

Glaciers, both past and present, are obviously the major basis of scenery within this park which straddles the continental divide in northern Montana. It is adjacent to Canada's Waterton Lakes National Park, and the two are now jointly designated as the Waterton-Glacier International Peace Park. Unusual geologic features are exhibited here, including not only glaciation, but sedimentation, metamorphism, volcanism, diastrophism, and erosion.

Glacier Park lies in the northern part of the Rocky Mountains, with the Lewis Range to the northeast, and the Livingston Range to the west. The elevation varies from about 3,000 feet to over 10,000 feet, with Mount Cleveland topping all other peaks at 10,448 feet.

A very common misconception is that the glaciers seen here are remnants of Pleistocene time, the so-called Great Ice Age. All of those actually once disappeared completely, and the present ones originated only some 4000 years ago.

Geologic History

The geology of Glacier Park has already been described in several excellent books, brochures, pamphlets, and magazines. Essentially, the rock strata are all of the Belt formation of upper Precambrian age. A great trough, or geosyncline, connecting the Arctic and Pacific Oceans from northwestern Canada to southern California and Arizona existed at this far-off time of half a billion years ago. Various sediments eroded from adjacent land areas accumulated in it, and as their thickness and weight increased, the bottom of the trough sank into a plastic-like earth. In this way, although the sea waters were actually shallow - probably never more than a thousand feet in depth - a total of at least 40,000 feet of sediments were locally deposited. This geosynclinal origin is common to all the world's major mountain ranges: the Rockies, Appalachians, Andes, Alps, Himalayas, etc.

49

Glacier Park shows six distinct and easily recognizable rock formations of marine origin, perhaps the best Precambrian sequence anywhere in the world. Lowest and oldest is the Altyn formation, a light buff magnesian or dolomite limestone, seen in the general base of the eastern front of the Lewis Range, also back of Many Glacier Hotel.

Mt. Grinnell and Grinnell Glacier as seen west of Lake Sherburne and Many Glacier Hotel.

Next higher is the Appekunny formation, composed of greenish shales metamorphosed to argillite, which show mud cracks and ripple marks as evidence of its shore-line origin. Tree-like dendritic markings of manganese dioxide, as in "moss" agates, are often discovered in its joint cracks. Seen from a distance, as along the Lewis Range, it may appear to have a purplish tinge.

The Grinnell formation conspicuously forms the reddish or maroon peaks most typical of Glacier Park. It is a red argillite, also of shallow-water origin as shown by its current and ripple marks, raindrop prints, mud cracks, etc., and includes intervening layers of white quartzite to a total thickness of 3000 feet. Grinnell Point, Red Eagle, and

Going-to-the-Sun Peaks are examples; one can also see it while passing through Ptarmigan Tunnel, or at the top of Redrock and Ptarmigan Falls.

Going-to-the-Sun Mountain (Elev. 9604 feet) — west of St. Mary's Lake.

The Siyeh formation, a cliff-forming limestone sometimes 4000 feet thick which may weather from a bluish-gray to a buff color, forms the main portions of Cleveland and Kintla Peaks, and caps other heights such as Gould, Siyeh, Grinnell, and the Garden Wall. It is this formation which most notably contains the cabbage-like fossil algae such as the genus *Cryptozoon,* meaning "hidden life," in a 60-foot bed containing their rounded masses. A few worm burrows are also recognized, but no other undoubted fossils are known in the park area. The Siyeh may be seen on the west side of Logan Pass and along the east face of Mount Wilbur.

The Shepard formation, yellowish-brown limy beds of shallow-water origin, can be distinguished on Summit, Swiftcurrent, Almost-a-Dog Mountains and others.

51

The sixth formation, the **Kintla**, is a less noticeable one since it occurs only at the tops of a few of the highest peaks, as around Boulder Pass, etc. Like the Grinnell, it is of bright red color, but its muddy composition contains cubical casts of ancient salt crystals which prove the aridity of that time, so causing evaporation of the water.

The Purcell lava flow was spread over the surface of the Siyeh formation while the latter was still submerged. Its underwater origin is indicated by its "pillow" structure, or smooth mounds sometimes 2 feet in diameter. It covers the surface of the so-called Granite Park, erroneously named.

Another distinctive formation of Glacier Park is a sill of dark, coarse-grained diorite intruded between the layers of the Siyeh formation as seen from Many Glacier Hotel on the face of the Garden Wall. This sill has a uniform thickness of about 100 feet, so it makes a convenient scale by which to judge the mountain heights. It is exposed along the highway on both sides of the summit of Logan Pass, and for about 200 yards along the Granite Park trail the sequence of the Siyeh limestone, the denser heat-altered zone, and the diorite itself can be seen at the surface.

Many more or less vertical dikes also cut through the Belt formations. These are of darker basaltic material which weathers easily, so that their presence is noted as a chute down the slope.

A long gap follows in the geological history of the region. Subsequent Beltian sediments, as well as Paleozoic or early Mesozoic ones, may have been formed only to have been eroded away. Fossiliferous sandstones, limestones, and shales of Cretaceous age, over 400 million years younger, lie immediately above; these are most accessible for study in the plains east of the park toward Browning and southeastward toward Augusta.

The Lewis Overthrust

During the Laramide (Rocky Mountain) mountain building, excessive deformation had folded the strata into an overturned anticline or arch, so that the eastern limb was uplifted as well as inverted, and crowded eastward for at least 20 miles. Thus older Precambrian or Paleozoic strata were placed immediately above the Cretaceous beds. This fault is known as the Lewis Overthrust.

Section of the Lewis Overthrust fault west of Augusta, Montana — Mississippian limestone thrust eastward over Cretaceous shale.

Erosion later removed much of this material, leaving isolated remnants which puzzled geologists because of the discrepancy between relative ages and positions. One of the best known is Chief Mountain (Elev. 9066 feet) which is a 1500-foot mass of Altyn limestone towering above the plains of black Cretaceous shale on the eastern park boundary, easily visible from Highway 17 between Babb, Montana, and the International Custom Stations.

A modern theory that overthrust faults do not move in response to a push from behind, but instead, slide downhill under the pull of gravity has been developed by geologists such as Dr. David D. Alt and Dr. Donald W. Hyndman, of the University of Montana. This is discussed in their "Rocks, Ice, and Water", Mountain Press Publishing Co., Missoula, Mont., 1973.

Subsequently in early Tertiary time there was a downward faulting of the western portion of this area, dropping it several thousand feet to form a lake basin now occupied by the North Fork of the Flathead River. By the Miocene and Pliocene Epochs the region had been deeply eroded, forming present valleys.

Chief Mountain — a remnant of Precambrian limestone overthrust eastward at least 12 miles over Cretaceous shale.

(From color slide by the writer)

Glaciation

With the cooling of the climate and accumulation of snow, the Pleistocene glaciers began their slow movement down the valleys, until all but the summits of the highest peaks were covered, and the forested regions were scraped clean. They probably extended into the plains on both sides of the park. After at least eight retreats and advances, a hot, dry time closed the Pleistocene so that 8000 years ago no glaciers remained. The next several thousand years saw the rebirth of the forests and the forming of today's glacial system. These probably reached maximum size as recently as the late 1880's, but have been shrinking since then. For example, Clements Glacier, which drained into both Hudson Bay and the Pacific Ocean, vanished about 1938, leaving a high ridge as a terminal moraine.

Glaciers are usually longer than their width, and found mainly above snowline, but these of Glacier Park differ in being rather short, and found in protected eastern or northern slopes below snowline, where wind carries the snow. Glacier .Park, then, is quite different from Alaskan glacial areas, and therefore especially deserving of appreciation.

WYOMING

DEVILS TOWER National Monument (Igneous Intrusive)

The Devils Tower area was the first of our National Monuments, created in 1906 during the administration of Pres. Theodore Roosevelt. (A monument emphasizes a single feature, rather than being an extensive scenic area.)

The Devils Tower is the tallest rock formation of its kind in the United States, 865 feet above its base in the Belle Fourche River valley. Its diameter tapers from about 1000 feet at its base to 275 feet at the top. The prominent middle and upper portions exhibit an extremely well-developed columnar structure, usually five-sided, with columns averaging 10 feet in diameter, some as large as 16 feet.

This spectacular column can be seen from a great distance, usually reached by way of State Route 24 from U.S. Highway 14, though the writer will never forget his first sight of it as he rode his bicycle along the dirt road from the Montana boundary. Suddenly, out there in the valley, it protruded in the light of the setting sun like the proverbial "sore thumb."

Devils Tower as seen from southern approach — an intrusive igneous mass of granitic type showing remarkable columnar jointing.

National Park Service

The tower has apparently served not only as a landmark, but as an object of some religious symbolism to the early Indian tribes. One well-known Indian name was "Mateo Tepee," meaning Grizzly Bear Lodge. Colonel Richard I. Dodge, who was the first to describe it in 1876 in his book, "The Black Hills," said that the Indians referred to it as "The Bad God's Tower," from whence came his translation.

Many Indian legends have been cited concerning it, the majority of which explain the fluted columns as vertical scratches made by the claws of a gigantic bear attacking one or more Indian maidens or warriors who miraculously escaped when the Great Spirit caused the rock to rise upward from the valley floor.

Geologists are not yet certain as to the origin of the structure. While there is no doubt as to the intrusive igneous character of the Devils Tower, the conditions through which it was formed are debatable. It is not basaltic, as are so many volcanic necks in the west. The average person would consider it a granite, as being light colored and coarsely grained, and many references avoid assigning an exact name or geologic time of formation; some describe it as a phonolite (nephelite-syenite) porphyry, which contains less quartz and more alkaline feldspars than a granite. It probably developed during the Tertiary volcanism of the western United States between 25 and 50 million years ago. Earlier beliefs had classed it as a volcanic neck, while others considered it as a portion of a much larger mass such as a stock or a laccolith, but latest studies suggest that it was intruded in approximately its present shape and size into the sediments surrounding it at a depth of perhaps 2500 feet. During the cooling process, columns were formed in the usual manner by contractual tensions, forming joints at obtuse angles, most commonly at 120°. Surrounding strata were removed later by erosion.

First climbed on July 4, 1893, by two ranchers who built a ladder by driving wooden stakes into a vertical crevice, it has been ascended several hundred times since. It is, however, an exhausting climb which requires experience and equipment, now to be attempted only under official permission from monument authorities.

GRAND TETON National Park
(Igneous Intrusive, Glaciation)

The Grand Teton Mountains south of Yellowstone National Park are another excellent example of nature's combinations of processes: volcanism, diastrophism, glaciation, and normal erosion. Of these, perhaps fault-block mountain building and glaciation are the best exemplified.

The granite peaks themselves are Precambrian in age, certain examples of the rocks having been dated by geophysicists back to 2½ billion years ago. Yet these crystalline veins are intruded into even older gneisses! As the mountains arose, erosion became more vigorous, cutting steep gorges in many directions.

Faulting occurred at the end of the Mesozoic Era and later, resulting in the sheer eastern face of the range. Grand Teton, 13,776 feet in elevation, towers over the flat valley of Jackson Hole. (The former Jackson Hole National Monument has been incorporated within Grand Teton National Park.)

The Three Tetons, as seen from Jenny Lake. Grand Teton (Elev. 13,766 feet) is a favorite ascent for climbers. (National Park Service)

Glaciation of the Pleistocene Epoch aided in the carving of the scenic features delighting the photographer's eye at present. The ice sheet which once occupied the valley melted away, but smaller glaciers returned to the mountain canyons as recently as 9000 years ago. Their moraines form natural dams for the many beautiful lakes hereabouts, notably Jackson Lake.

Retreat of the ice finally exposed the typical geologic effects it had caused: cirques at the heads of U-shaped mountain valleys, the sharply cut spires (Matterhorns) forming majestic peaks, and glacial debris covering valley floors, perfecting the flatness of the surfaces.

A concluding fact of interest to the many readers who enjoyed Owen Wister's *"The Virginian"* is that Mystic Isle (sometimes unofficially and locally called "Honeymoon Island"), enclosed within beautiful Leigh Lake of this glacial group, is said to be the lovely site mentioned as his selection for the first night's encampment with his bride.

Mount Moran, reflected in Jackson Lake, the largest lake in the National Park. Leigh Lake is southward from here, and Jenny Lake farther southward, almost opposite Grand Teton. (National Park Service)

YELLOWSTONE National Park (Igneous Intrusive and Extrusive, Glaciation)

Not only is Yellowstone our first and largest (3472 square miles, or 2,221,773 acres) National Park, also one of the most popular, but its assemblage of earth phenomena is more varied than those found in other national areas.

Early history of the Park's exploration by John Colter, a former soldier with the Lewis and Clark Expedition, later accounts by Jim Bridger and associates, then the three-man expedition of 1869, followed in 1870 by the Washburn-Langford-Doane Expedition have been related in the previous discussion "Origin of the National Park System." These finally led to the Congressional Act of March 1, 1872, under the administration of President Ulysses S. Grant, which set aside the region "for the benefit and enjoyment of the people," as stated on the entrance arch at Gardiner, Montana. (See page xi) Now more than two million visitors each year come to see Yellowstone National Park, and few, if any, have been disappointed.

Geologic History

The earliest rocks of two or three billion years ago were igneous types, like granite, as elsewhere. These formed land areas which became subjected to erosion, producing sedimentaries, with these in turn being metamorphosed by igneous intrusion and mountain-building diastrophism into gneisses and schists which, though not exposed within Park boundaries, are known in adjoining states.

During Paleozoic time, advances and retreats of shallow seas created various formations of sandstones, shales, and limestones. There was less crustal movement in the west during this era than in eastern states, where the Appalachian Mountains were uplifted and folded about 225 million years ago.

The Mesozoic Era brought further successive sea invasions in the region, with marine limestones and shales containing invertebrate fossils, and swamp deposits such as the Morrison formation, widely known in Wyoming and Utah for its reptilian fossil bones. During the Jurassic and Cretaceous Periods great batholithic intrusions occurred in the Sierra Nevada, Rockies, and parts of those ranges bordering Yellowstone Park, such as the Absarokas, Gallatins, and the Tetons. Late Cretaceous sediments covered the metamorphic basement rocks, but even these are exposed only in a few places, such as along the Snake River and its tributaries in the south-central Park, but otherwise covered by much later volcanics and glacial gravels. Here, too, can be seen the folds and faults of the Laramide orogeny which formed the Rockies. For example, a large eroded anticline is visible along the road between the northeast entrance and Mammoth Hot Springs.

During the Cenozoic Era, the region was high above sea level throughout Tertiary time, and many Eocene volcanoes erupted about 50 million years ago, forming major portions of the Absaroka and Washburn Ranges and part of the Gallatin Range. The Absaroka sequence of volcanics, comprising about 4200 feet in thickness, is especially notable. These consist mostly of andesite, a finely-crystalline igneous rock of intermediate composition, and some basalt, which is darker because of higher iron-magnesian content. Eruptions were intermittent, with explosive activities producing bombs, cinders, and ash which became wind-blown over vast areas of the western states.

At the time of this Eocene volcanism, all of Yellowstone had become a gently rolling plateau, covered by several thousand feet of lavas, breccias, and ash, and drained by slowly flowing, winding streams. The surface was not more than a few thousand feet above sea level, and fossil animals and plants indicate warmer climate prevailed than at present.

Fossil forests are well known in the Park. Specimen Ridge Fossil Forest, which is a portion of one of the largest petrified tree areas in the world, may be visited by an all-day hike from Tower Junction. Trees here are usually still upright, unlike those scattered horizontally in Petrified Forest, Arizona. Another interesting occurrence, often missed by Park visitors, is Amethyst Cliff, across the valley from the northeast entrance road near Lamar. Here the Lamar River has cut through a section of about 2000 feet of volcanic and sedimentary beds in alternate layers in which

27 distinct fossil forests are visible. These include many species of trees now typical of southeastern and southern states, such as walnut, chestnut, oak, redwood, maple, sycamore, and magnolia.

The later Tertiary Epochs, Oligocene and Miocene, are not represented by deposits anywhere in the Park, and the Pliocene seems to have been a time of major erosion. Some uplift with faulting also occurred toward the close of the Tertiary. The Gallatin River region and the Teton Range were tilted upwards, while the Jackson Hole region slipped downward along a fault on the eastern face of the Tetons, forming their remarkably steep face, or scarp. Stream erosion increased with this rise in elevation, and by the end of the Tertiary Period Yellowstone was probably a region of deep canyons separating table lands.

The Yellowstone Caldera development at the beginning of the Quaternary Period, some two million years ago, is a significant part of Yellowstone's geologic history. Two magma chambers a few thousand feet below the surface acted as a huge double reservoir of molten rock, and after preliminary arching and cracking of the surface, the material blasted out in what must have been one of the greatest volcanic explosions in all of earth history, similar to the far lesser one of Krakatoa in 1883. Pumice, ash, and debris formed flows and airborne dust spread over central and western United States. Old canyons were filled, and most highlands were buried, except for such as Mount Washburn and Bunsen Peak. Some lava flows occurred, but most of the hot material welded itself together into the Yellowstone tuff, with the mineral composition of rhyolite.

The removal of these hundreds of cubic miles of molten rock from subsurface chambers caused collapse of their roofs, creating a caldera several thousand feet deep. At present it has been more or less filled by thick lava flows, so is less noticeable. Its boundaries were approximately the Washburn Range slopes on the north, the Flathead and Red Mountains near Yellowstone Lake on the south, while the eastern edge of the lake corresponds roughly to the eastern rim of the caldera. An inner caldera, similar to Crater Lake, Oregon, was formed less than 200,000 years ago. This now is occupied by the West Thumb portion of the lake.

As molten rock again rose in the chambers, domes formed in the caldera floor, one near Old Faithful, the other east of Hayden Valley. Ring fracture zones encircled the pit, through which lava flows flooded the floor and ultimately filled the caldera. Some flowed out through fractures in the rim, of which Obsidian Cliff (Jim Bridger's "Mountain of Glass"), to be seen north of Norris Geyser Basin, is one example.

About 30 different flows comprise this Plateau Rhyolite, creating the present undulating surface of central Yellowstone. Some basalt flows also occurred, as seen in the vertical columns near Tower Falls. The last of these date back to about 60-75,000 years ago, with the subsurface heat forces indicated afterward only by the everpresent hot water and steam.

Glaciation

Glaciation occurred at least three times in the Yellowstone area, with the last (Pinedale) phase, existing between 8,500 and 25,000 years ago. The Pinedale icefield formed in the Absaroka Range and flowed northward down the Yellowstone valley into the lake basin. An icefield also formed in mountains north of the Park, sending tongues into the lower Yellowstone and Lamar valleys, while small valley glaciers developed in the Absaroka Range to the east, and in the Gallatin Range to the northwest. Convergence of these ice masses during the 10,000 years following produced a mountain of ice over the Yellowstone Lake basin, perhaps 3000 feet thick. The ice moved across the Grand Canyon of the Yellowstone, but did not flow down it, evidenced by the present V-shape of stream erosion rather than the U-shape of glaciation. About 90% of the Yellowstone area was covered with ice 15,000 years ago, but largely melted away during the next 3000 years. The last of the valley glaciers disappeared about 8,500 years ago.

An interesting glacial feature is the giant "erratic" of Precambrian gneiss which lies among trees beside the road toward Inspiration Point on the north side of the Grand Canyon. It measures about 24 ft. by 20 ft. by 18 ft., and probably weighs 500 tons or more. Yet it is at least 15 miles from the nearest outcrop of gneiss — to the north-northeast — and hence must have been moved by the glacial ice-sheet.

Glacial erratic boulder — on north side of the Grand Canyon of the Yellowstone, adjacent to the highway. (From color slide by the writer)

Stream drainage in the park flows in two general directions, with the continental divide looping across the highway twice between Old Faithful and West Thumb. At one place Isa Lake lies on the divide, with outlets to both east and west.   One system follows the Yellowstone, Madison, and Gallatin Rivers eastward, the other travels westward via the Snake and Columbia Rivers.

The **Grand Canyon of the Yellowstone,** so frequently photographed, was created during several stages within the last two million or more years, including ancestral cutting into the Absaroka sequence of volcanics, filling of the former channel by ash-flow tuffs, re-carving of the new stream bed, and formation of a lake which filled much of the south-central portion of the old caldera and finally spilled over into the canyon.

Waterfalls are common in the Park; of which Upper and Lower Falls of the Yellowstone, Gibbon Falls, and Tower Falls are best known. Both falls of the Yellowstone are due

Lower Falls of the Yellowstone River — 308 feet high. It falls over the contact between a harder mass of rhyolite upstream than the softer rhyolite below.

to the contact between hard, darker rhyolite upstream and softer, eroded rhyolite downstream. (Many textbooks of past years have cited Lower Yellowstone Falls as a good example of a river passing over a resistant basaltic dike, but in recent studies by the U.S.G.S. the correction cited above is made.) Gibbon Falls developed over a fault scarp in the Yellowstone Tuff, and Tower Falls is an example of the tributary being unable to erode as fast as the parent stream, and therefore falling over a cliff of Absaroka volcanic breccia and conglomerate.

Final filling of the canyon with glacial ice, then melting of this followed by more downward erosion within the last 150-200,000 years has produced its modern appearance. The yellow coloration of the weathered rhyolite in its walls is said to have been the origin of the name "Yellowstone."

Hot springs, geysers, mudpots, and **fumaroles** are various forms of thermal action within the park. Subsurface temperatures have not cooled measurably during the last hundred years while records have been kept. Heat from buried magma is transmitted into adjoining rock, into which surface water has seeped through the joints and fissures to perhaps 5000-10,000 feet in depth. Here the water becomes heated far above its normal surface boiling point because of the pressure of the water column. Simultaneously, minerals are dissolved from adjoining rocks to be redeposited at the surface.

Mineral deposits from dissolved substances are formed around hot water areas. In most places these are siliceous, of "sinter," or "geyserite," because of water having passed through rhyolite; in the Mammoth Hot Springs region, where

Hymen Terrace - Mammoth Hot Springs. One of many such formed of a porous limestone, or "travertine," deposited by hot sub-surface waters.

thick limestones occur, deposits are of calcareous "travertine." Liberty Cap is such a deposit, 40 feet high, from an
extinct hot spring, perhaps 14,000 years in forming.

Hot water algae color the terraced surfaces green,
brown, or yellow, existing as microscopic plant life thriving
in water as hot as 170° F.

Liberty Cap — Mammoth Hot Springs. A conical deposit from an
extinct hot spring, 40 feet high, formed of "travertine."

Geysers differ from hot springs in that they erupt at
more or less regular intervals. Hot springs flow steadily,
whether boiling or not. There are at least 200 geysers in
Yellowstone Park, more than in any other single location in
the world.

Necessary features are: (1) a nearly vertical tube, descending a few hundred feet below the surface, (2) side storage chambers as reservoirs for water while being heated, and (3) connections farther downward through narrow tubes leading to deep sources of water amid the heated rocks adjacent to magmas.

The cycle of eruption includes (1) the recovery or recharge stage, in which tube and reservoirs are refilled primarily from surface waters and heated nearly to their boiling point at existing water column pressures; (2) the preliminary eruption stage, in which many gas bubbles collect and clog emission of water; (3) the stage of full eruption,

Old Faithful Geyser — average interval between eruptions of 65 minutes, height about 125 feet. Upper Geyser Basin. (National Park Service)

beginning with a slight spurting of hot water from the vent, thus relieving pressure below and lowering the boiling point, so that large amounts of waters in the tube and side reservoirs flash abruptly into steam; and (4) the stage when eruption ceases, steam flows for a while, and the cycle begins anew.

Old Faithful is of course the best known of all geysers, with eruption intervals averaging 65 minutes apart, although they have varied between 33 and 96 minutes. The eruption lasts for 3 or 4 minutes, throwing water up to 170 feet high.

Some geysers, like the Minuteman, may erupt very frequently, while others such as Grotto, Castle, Teakettle, Riverside, and Lone Star are less predictable, erupting at intervals of several hours. Still others may stay quiet for days or weeks. The Excelsior Geyser, now dormant or extinct, is considered to have been Yellowstone's largest, formerly discharging a column of water and steam 200-300 feet high for 4-15 minutes. Seismic Geyser is one which was

Grotto Geyser — irregularly predictable as to eruption intervals. Notable for its cavernous appearance, due to multi-outlet system. Upper Geyser Basin.

Castle Geyser — irregularly predictable as to eruption intervals, usually hours or days. Upper Geyser Basin.

Teakettle Geyser — minor eruptions, more nearly a hot spring. Characterized by its unusually symmetrical "travertine" rim. Upper Geyser Basin.

a result of the Hebgen Lake quake in the Madison River valley, 12 miles north of West Yellowstone, near midnight August 17, 1959. A resultant landslide crashed across Rock Creek campground, injuring many, and burying 19 unrecovered bodies.

Mudpots occur where the hot water is inadequate, and mixes with clay etc. to form material of various tints — black, gray, cream, or white, or even reddish from iron compounds. The Fountain Paint Pots of the Lower Geyser Basin are one example, to be seen near Fountain Geyser, while others occur at West Thumb near Fishing Cone.

Mud volcanoes are formed when the mud is so thick that it forms pellets which collect into mounds, the best known being between Canyon Village and Fishing Bridge.

Mud geysers are similar, but have their craters filled with sulfurous, fuming mud in a state of constant motion. It may choke the vent so as to cause steam pressure to accumulate, finally resulting in an eruption.

Fumaroles, or steam vents, are found where ground water is scarce, and the steaming fumes emerge violently at high temperatures. The Black Growler and Hurricane Vent are to be observed in the Norris Geyser Basin.

U T A H

ARCHES National Park (Erosion)

Northernmost of a series of arches and natural bridges is Arches National Park, raised to that status in 1971 from its former designation as a National Monument. Its location is near the city of Moab, Utah. A vast assortment of arches may be seen here, double as well as single, newly formed as well as fallen in, thick and thin, high and low.

Most of these can be reached by automobile, with only short hikes of a mile or so necessary to view the remainder. Landscape Arch, with a span of 291 feet, may be the world's largest.

Landscape Arch — probably the world's largest with a span of 291 feet.
(National Park Service)

Arches and natural bridges are of very different origin - a feature often unrecognized by visitors because of their similar appearance. Arches have been eroded by wind through fins of rock left between erosion of joints, nearly always in sandstone. Natural bridges, however, have been cut by the erosion of meandering streams. Here the arches

71

have been cut into the 300-foot Entrada sandstone which overlies the Carmel formation, while the Navajo sandstone underlies the one last-named. All are of Jurassic age.

Delicate Arch, as its name would indicate, surmounts a sandstone block and is one of the thinner ones probably soon to collapse. The Double O Arch, Tunnel Arch, and many others, are self-descriptive.

Delicate Arch -- considered by National Park authorities as perhaps the most beautiful of all. (National Park Service)

The **Moab Fault** is worthy of mention. The Jurassic strata on the eastern side of the valley, from which the highway ascends to the plateau of Entrada sandstone, are not to be seen on the other side. There the lowest of geologic formations, beside the highway, is the Hermosa, a Pennsylvanian marine fossiliferous stratum. Above it lie the Cutler-Rico, the Moenkopi, the Chinle (notable in the Painted Desert) and above all, a cliff of Wingate Sandstone, all of Triassic age. Layers which once lay above these have been eroded away, as have still others which overlay the Jurassic Entrada on the eastern side.

Geologists estimate that about 6 million years ago a crack developed along the line of the highway, and the monument side sank at least 2600 feet, thus bringing the younger strata to coincident level with the older ones on the western side of the valley.

BRYCE CANYON National Park   (Erosion)

Bryce Canyon, in southwestern Utah between Capitol Reef and Zion, is admired by many visitors as presenting perhaps the most vividly colored natural formations anywhere in the world. Truly, words are inadequate in attempting any description; only an accurate color photograph can begin to portray it. The Paiute Indian name for the region translates as: "red rocks standing like men in a bend-shaped canyon."

First, Bryce is not a true canyon with major walls on both sides, but the cracked and gullied eastern face of the Pausaugunt Plateau, formed as a fault escarpment into which water could form crevices, carve shapes, and develop minute details of rock sculpture. The fault block contains about 2000 feet of limestone with some silt and sand, known as the Pink Cliffs formation, a portion of the Wasatch limestone. It is a fairly recent Cenozoic formation, deposited during the early Tertiary Period of about 55 million years ago. This was millions of years later than the somewhat similarly eroded sediments of the Zion and Grand Canyons, although like them, the rocks may have been lifted many thousands of feet above the level of the seas which had formed them.

In fact, these three scenic sites illustrate the major divisions of earth history. Bryce Canyon represents the Cenozoic Age of Mammals; Zion Canyon includes formations of Mesozoic time, that of the Age of Reptiles; Grand Canyon portrays in its side walls the strata of Paleozoic time, dominated by invertebrates and fishes, while the inner gorge digs deeply into the ancient metamorphosed sediments and intrusive granites and gneisses of two or three billion years ago.

The gorgeous variegated colors of red, pink, orange, and yellow, together with narrow stripings of lavender, brown, and gray are due to mixtures of different oxides of manganese and iron. From Rainbow Point, near the south end of the Park, the formation zigzags for 30 miles toward the northeastern horizon, over an area of about 56 square miles along the rim. Valley floors are uniformly covered with gray sage, while dark evergreen forests top the mesa.

Originally formed as layers of sediment in inland seas and lakes, mountain-building pressures then forced these blocks upward between major fault lines, forming flat-topped mesas. These were rapidly worn away by wind, rain, and frost activity, producing a variety of shapes because of differences in hardness vertically and horizontally. Spires, pinnacles, figures, and windows exist by the thousand, as indicated by such imaginative names as Silent City, Fairy Temple, Queen Victoria, Three Wise Men, Thor's Hammer, the Alligator, and scores of others.

Foot trails for camera-packing hikers are numerous, both along the rim and down into the valley. These exist in a variety of slopes and lengths suitable to degrees of walking ability, thus adding to the general desirability of Bryce Canyon as a vacationer's paradise.

Silent City, seen from across Bryce Canyon. Erosional spires of pink Tertiary limestone. (National Park Service)

CANYONLANDS National Park   (Erosion)

Canyonlands is an irregular area in southeastern Utah which includes portions of the Colorado and Green Rivers and also their confluence. It is a region of rugged, undisturbed scenery, generally accessible only by four-wheel drive vehicles, particularly so for Angel Arch in the extreme southeast corner.

There are three general levels in the park. The highest is the comparatively flat-topped "Island in the Sky" toward the north. Cliffs drop a thousand feet or more from its rim to another relatively level plateau, the White Rim. This likewise terminates in still another thousand feet of cliffs, the Needles Area, dropping to the entrenched rivers below.

Chesler Park is a grassy enclosure of about a thousand acres, encircled by sandstone pinnacles, some equalling a ten-story building in height. These have been eroded along joints in the Cedar Mesa sandstone of the Permian Cutler formation. To the west, the sandstone has been faulted into "grabens," or sunken valleys.

Needles Area of Chesler Park, the lower group of cliffs which drop to the Colorado River below.   (National Park Service)

The White Rim section overlying these is likewise of Permian age, the White Rim sandstone, while the uppermost plateau surface is of Wingate sandstone of the Glen Canyon group, which includes the uncertain boundary between the Triassic and Jurassic Periods.

Cataract Canyon, immediately below the junction of the Colorado and Green Rivers, provides an adventure of running rapids suitable only for experienced persons.

Below the canyon, the Colorado River expands into Lake Powell, the result of water stored behind Glen Canyon dam near Page, Arizona. A boat trip on Lake Powell now brings the visitor to a landing only about half a mile from Rainbow Bridge, Utah, formerly accessible only via a desert overland trail.

Upheaval Dome must not be omitted. Located in the Island in the Sky area, it appears to be an immense crater, perhaps 4500 feet across and 1600 feet deep. It is not at all volcanic in origin, but appears to be a circular anticline, or upward folding of the strata. Not yet fully understood, it probably is a large salt dome underlain by an intrusion of magma below.

CAPITOL REEF National Park (Diastrophism)

Capitol Reef in south-central Utah was so-named because of a doubly interesting word origin. Early sailors who followed the Australian gold rush described the gold bearing ridges with their nautical term of "reefs," and the name was carried into American mining as referring to any rocky barrier. Second, the cap rock of the area, the gray or white Navajo sandstone of Triassic-Jurassic age, weathers into domes resembling those of many state capitol buildings.

Capitol Reef was indeed a barrier to travel. The great Waterpocket Fold, an upward-faulted portion of the earth's crust, extends for about 100 miles from Thousand Lake Mountain in a southeast direction toward the Colorado River, and about 70 miles of this is included in the national monument. Waterpockets themselves are the result of swirling, sediment-laden waters boring out pockets or tanks in the stream bed adjacent to irregularities of strata, as at the lower end of Capitol Gorge.

Only three canyons permitted travel through the reef, which is highest toward the northwest, sinking into the ground at the other end. One of these is the Fremont River Canyon, the current route for automobile travel. Capitol Gorge, occupying a stream valley probably formed before the uplift, was a dangerously narrow route through which the covered wagons of the 1880's made their hazardous passage. At the end of the Grand Wash road, a a major scenic attraction of the monument, a hike of 1½ miles brings one to The Narrows, where a valley width of only 16 feet separates the 1000 foot cliffs.

Another narrow passage is half a mile from the eastern end of Capitol Gorge, where carved inscriptions made by the early pioneers may be seen, the earliest date being 1871.

During threat of rain storms, the gate to Capitol Gorge may be closed by the monument authorities because of danger from flash floods, and visitors are warned not to park in the bottom of the wash for this reason.

Geologically, the sandstone cliff has been described as an extremely fine example of a monocline formed by crustal uplift. The topmost layer is the almost white Navajo sandstone of the Jurassic Period, eroded into various domes, arches, and cones. Next below is the Wingate sandstone, perhaps 600 feet thick, of a dark red or chocolate brown color. Many geologists consider the Wingate as marking the boundary between the Jurassic and Triassic Periods. The Triassic Chinle shale, in variegated bands changing from gray-green at the bottom to maroon or purple at the top, underlies that. The floor of the canyon is composed of dark red Moenkopi shale, often showing shallow-water ripple marks, together with fossil amphibian or reptilian footprints. These formations are all commonly known throughout the southwest. They also occur in Zion National Park in Utah, the Painted Desert and Petrified Forest of Arizona, and into Colorado and New Mexico.

Erosion has been effective amid these soft formations in the arid climate, carving fanciful figures into the thin, colorful layers. The Castle, Chimney Rock, Golden Throne, and Egyptian Temple are among the typically descriptive names assigned to such shapes. Hickman Natural Bridge, stream-cut like many others in Utah, stands 72 feet high with a width of 133 feet.

The uplift or folding of this area took place toward the close of the Cretaceous Period, associated with the general birth of the modern Rocky Mountains.

Capitol Gorge wagon road near The Narrows, through which pioneer wagons of the 1800's crossed the Waterpocket Fold

(From color slide by the writer)

CEDAR BREAKS National Monument (Erosion)

Cedar Breaks is located to the north-northeast of Zion National Park, and west of Bryce Canyon National Park, but much smaller in size than either of these. It is accessible via State Highway 14, either from Cedar City to the west or Long Valley Junction to the east.

The geology is very similar to that of Bryce Canyon, both being eroded from the Pink Cliffs formation. Cedar Breaks has been formed as an amphitheater on the 10,000 foot Markagunt Plateau. In addition, volcanic flows of only a few thousand years ago have poured from fissures in the eastern portion, also to the north of Cedar Breaks where Brianhead is a major example, just beyond the park boundary.

Eroded cliffs of Tertiary Wasatch limestone, with Brianhead — a volcanic flow — visible in the distance. (National Park Service)

The Wasatch limestone, of which the Pink Cliffs formation is a colorful portion, was a limy ooze deposited in shallow Eocene lakes near sea level about 55 million years ago. As in Bryce Canyon, a general uplift and development of fault blocks occurred during the Pliocene, dated at about 13 million years before the present. The Cedar Breaks amphitheater is an escarpment facing westward, with rims on the north, east, and south.

Erosion has produced ridges and other shapes, although isolated spires are almost absent. The colors are claimed by some to be even more varied than those of Bryce Canyon.

There is, however, considerable vegetative difference between Cedar Breaks and Bryce because of the variance in elevation — more than 10,000 feet within Cedar Breaks, and an average of about 8,500 feet for Bryce. One noticeable difference is that Cedar Breaks is superior in abundance of annual wildflowers. These include the marshmarigold, columbine, larkspur, Indian paintbrush, lupine, and many more.

NATURAL BRIDGES National Monument (Erosion)

Three large natural bridges are to be seen in this small area of southeastern Utah. The largest one, Sipapu, with a span of 268 feet, is surpassed only by the gigantic Rainbow Bridge farther south.

The bridges are located in two tributary canyons of the Colorado River, those of the White and Armstrong Rivers, about 60 miles upstream from Rainbow Bridge.

Like the latter, these were formed by the production of narrow partitions between bends of meandering rivers, which swing across their valleys with erosive forces much increased by uplift of the area. Sooner or later the current, constantly impinging against the walls of its valley, will tunnel out a short-cut channel between the meanders. All of these are in the Cedar Mesa sandstone of Permian age, which is much older than the Jurassic Navajo sandstone.

Sipapu Bridge, with a 268 foot span, cut through a meander wall of White River. (National Park Service)

81

Interestingly, these three bridges well exemplify the phases of life of a natural bridge, as of a stream, by using human life terms. Most youthful is Kachina Bridge, huge and bulky, with White River's flood waters still enlarging the gap. The largest, Sipapu Bridge farther up in White Canyon, is maturely symmetrical and well formed. The river now has minimum cutting effect upon its gap as the span is based too far from the stream for continual widening. Owachomo Bridge, the smallest, is in a tributary valley, Armstrong Canyon, and is not visible from monument headquarters. Stream erosion has entirely ceased here, and only wind, frost, and rain can affect it further. Being in its old age phase, it is less likely to endure than the others. In fact, farther up White Canyon from Sipapu Bridge can be seen the remains of a former fourth bridge, long since collapsed.

Comparative dimensions of the three bridges are, in feet:

	Height	Span	Width	Thickness
Sipapu	220	268	31	53
Kachina	210	206	44	93
Owachomo	106	180	27	9

Great Goosenecks of the San Juan River

This southeastern Utah State Park area contains the classic example of stream erosion in entrenched meanders, pictured in almost all geology textbooks. Muley Point on the plateau, where this photograph was taken, is 1200 feet above river level. These are the original conditions from which natural bridges may develop, although none have yet done so here due to the comparatively minimal time involved.

Goosenecks of the San Juan River — the most famous example of entrenchment of meanders in the world.   (From color slide by the writer)

Natural bridges can be formed by other geological processes. Virginia's famous Natural Bridge was created by collapse of the ceiling over a limestone cave. In Tonto National Monument, Arizona, a travertine deposit became undercut by the stream. Others develop along a coast line due to wave action on jointed cliffs.

RAINBOW BRIDGE National Monument (Erosion)

Practically everyone possessing the slightest interest in the natural scenic wonders of the west has heard of Rainbow Bridge. Zane Grey's novel, "The Rainbow Trail," uses this as a major environment in the story.

Yet until only the last few years in which Glen Canyon Dam and Lake Powell have been built, Rainbow Bridge was among the less commonly visited areas under the National Park Service administration.

For a long time it was known only by legend even to most of the Navajo and Paiute Indians living nearby. They referred to it as "Nonnezoshi Biko," or the Stone Rainbow.

In 1909 two separate parties of explorers led respectively by Dr. Byron Cummings of the University of Utah and W. B. Douglas, a government surveyor, started out to investigate the rumors of such a great stone arch in the Navajo Mountain region. During their search, the two parties became united, and after several days of difficult travel through canyons filled by boulders and junipers, if not water, while guided by Nasja Begay, son of a Paiute chief, a curve along the creek channel suddenly brought them to the most beautiful, also the largest, of all stone arches ever discovered.

For years afterward a 14-mile trail from Rainbow Lodge in Arizona, or a 24-mile trail from Navajo Trading Post in Utah, traversed only by horseback or on foot, discouraged all but the most experienced desert travelers. Now daily boat trips under Canyon Tours, Inc. make the 50-mile run northward from Wahweap, or southward from Halls Crossing via Lake Powell through Forbidding Canyon to the marina on the banks of Bridge Creek. In 1967 the hike from here to the base of Rainbow Bridge was about a mile long, over a sandy path climbing perhaps 150 feet.

As rising waters of the Colorado River gradually fill Lake Powell to its planned maximum, the walk from the boat dock in Rainbow Bridge Canyon will be lessened. A personally written letter from Art Greene, Jr. of Wahweap Lodge and Marina Canyon Tours, Inc. informs the writer that as of November 6, 1972, this distance is just under one half mile, and will eventually be less than one quarter of a mile. "At no time," he writes, "will the water cover any part of Rainbow Bridge." He encloses a clipping covering the last week of October in which it is recorded that the lake elevation rose from 3608.40 feet to 3609.22 feet — an average increase in depth of 0.13 of an inch per day.

Entering trail up Bridge Canyon. The foreground, Aztec Creek in Forbidding Canyon, is now flooded by rising waters of Lake Powell.
(National Park Service)

Rainbow Bridge crosses Bridge Canyon with a 278-foot span at a height of 309 feet, sufficient to enclose the dome of the Capitol Building of Washington, D.C. It is thus the largest in the world, as well as the most symmetrical and colorful. Its top is 42 feet in thickness and 33 feet in width, sufficient for an average highway.

Rainbow Bridge — largest, most symmetrical and colorful of such in the world. Its span is 278 feet long and 309 feet high.

Many similar bridges have been cut by erosive forces of uplifted meandering streams, such as those in Utah's Natural Bridges and Canyonlands National Monuments, also Virginia's famous Natural Bridge near Staunton, originally surveyed by George Washington and purchased by Thomas Jefferson from King George III, but Rainbow Bridge surpasses them all.

The bridge has been carved through the Navajo sandstone, a soft, thick, dune formation of early Jurassic age, overlying the Kayenta formation of the canyon floor. Sweeping meanders developed upon this were deepened after the uplift of the Colorado Plateau, also the intrusive elevation of Navajo Mountain. Fins and necks of solid rocks were left between the curves of the stream, finally to be cut through by pebbles and sand until a direct channel was produced at the site of such bridges. Wind, frost, and solution of cementing materials continued to form the symmetrical shape of Rainbow Bridge, as elsewhere in the world.

TIMPANOGOS CAVE National Monument (Ground Water)

Timpanogos is one of the smaller cave systems under the National Park Service, but it does have its own individual beauties, particularly the notable development of helictites upon the walls, said by some to be the finest of such known displays in this country.

There are really three distinct caverns, now connected by man-made tunnels. Hansen Cave was named after its discoverer in 1887, while Middle and Timpanogos were found in 1921. The last name is based upon an Indian word meaning "rock river."

The monument is located on Utah 80, east of U.S. 50, 89, and 91 between Salt Lake City and Provo. The caves lie upon a slope of Mount Timpanogos in the Wasatch Mountains, 1065 feet upward from the floor of American Fork Canyon. A visitor center, museum, and auditorium have been constructed here. A 1½ mile trail, usually snow-covered between November 1 and April 30, leads from the visitor center to the cave entrance.

Geologic History

The caves were apparently created as a result of water erosion through faulted rocks broken by the elevation of the Wasatch Range. Precambrian rocks are known in the region, although a break in the geologic record exists from the Cambrian to the Mississippian Period. The caves were formed in the Madison limestone, or according to some geologists, in the Deseret limestone immediately above, both of Mississippian age. Fractures occurred long after deposition of cave formations had been accomplished, as illustrated.

At first a fault zone of weakened rock material formed a reservoir of greater width than the channel of the American Fork River which was flowing then at the level of the cave formation. As the debris was carried downstream, a tunnel developed which was finally enlarged into caves. Rapid erosion of the canyon carried the valley floor below cave level, where the water found another drainage route, or was lessened because of decreased rainfall.

The cave formations are varied, also highly colorful, ranging in size from the small crystals and finger-like stalactites to larger deposits, and including colors from white through cream to yellow, brown, red, blue, or lavender due to iron and other mineral impurities in the calcium carbonate. Timpanogos is a "live" cave, meaning that deposition of dripstone (flowstone) draperies and other formations which began after the stream water ceased to flow is still taking place by ground water seepage.

Cave formations broken by an earthquake before the discovery of the cave.   (National Park Service)

ZION National Park (Erosion)

Zion National Park is sometimes considered as our best national example of a deep, narrow, vertically walled canyon which can be easily reached by highways. It is located in southwestern Utah, traversed by Utah 15 between Interstate 15 and U.S. 89. The mile-long Zion-Mt. Carmel tunnel is an interesting feature of this route.

The Zion area consists of a portion of the Kolob Plateau cut deeply by the swiftly flowing, silt laden North Fork of the Virgin River, which thus embodies the two main needs for rapid valley erosion: velocity and abrasive material. The valley gradient is about 50-70 feet per mile, almost ten times that of the Colorado River in Grand Canyon!

The Great White Throne — symbolical to many of Zion National Park. Formed of Jurassic Navajo sandstone, 2450 feet above the river.

(National Park Service)

89

Geologic History

Some compare the region with Yosemite, which may be true in a broad sense. The geologic contrast, however, is extreme, when one does consider the glaciated granites of Yosemite with their counterpart walls of stream-eroded soft formations of Zion. Both causes, though, have resulted in tributary hanging valleys above the main channel.

Three principal landscapes may be described: there is the pale, cross-bedded Navajo sandstone of Clear Creek valley, notably forming Checkerboard Mesa; second, there is Zion Canyon itself, carved into the Navajo sandstone with the Great White Throne towering 2450 feet above the river; and third, there is the Kolob region to the northwest, with its eight finger-like canyons. This was once reserved as Zion National Monument in 1937, but in 1956 its 76 square miles were added to Zion National Park.

The geologic sequence is typical of the southwest. The Carmel and Navajo sandstones were formed as desert sands in the Jurassic Period, some 150 million years ago, as evidenced by the aeolian cross-bedding. These were preceded by the Triassic Chinle-Kayenta-Wingate group, heretofore mentioned. Submersion beneath shallow invading seas, followed by uplift, occurred several times until in the Tertiary part of the Cenozoic Era, only about 13 million years ago, a general uplift of many thousands of feet caused fault-block breakage along several lines, increased erosive power of streams, and so created waterfalls from the tributary hanging valleys. The great Hurricane fault, reaching a maximum displacement of 8000 feet near Kanarraville, is the most famous one.

Continued erosion by the rushing water of the formerly sluggish rivers finally exposed the lower formations, beautifully portraying the sequential events of past geologic ages.

It is true that in general the continents of the world now exist at a higher elevation than at many times in the past, and this factor is responsible for the great number of scenic beauties so frequently photographed every day.

UTAH – COLORADO

DINOSAUR National Monument (Paleontology – Erosion)

One of the greatest single assemblages of fossil dinosaur bones found anywhere in the world was discovered in northeastern Utah east of Vernal by Dr. Earl Douglass of the Pittsburgh Carnegie Museum. The original 80 acres of the fossil area was declared a National Monument in 1915, to be followed in 1938 by the addition of 326 square miles of canyon country carved by the Green River within Colorado and Utah, and the Yampa River, its Colorado tributary.

The rock formation is the Morrison of Jurassic age, more famous for its dinosaur bones in Wyoming and adjacent states than any other rocky stratum. The sediments, mostly gray, shaly sandstones, were apparently deposited under swampy conditions, the preferred habitat for the heavy-bodied reptiles. The multitude of scattered bones seems to have accumulated as the dead bodies washed against a sandbar in a stream bed, these including some forms which may have been dry-land types.

About 5000 feet of sediments were next formed as overlying deposits, during which time the bones became replaced by silica. Uplift of the region during the Laramide (Rocky Mountain) Revolution caused subsequent erosion, exposing again the bones of these creatures who existed 150 million years ago.

The widely-ranging race of dinosaurs, whose existence continued through the next, or Cretaceous Period, may have come to extinction by falling volcanic ash, or as suggested by some, by some bacterial plague. Or again, as with other prehistoric fauna, evolutionary developments may have merely caused the race to reach a climax, then subside into oblivion. Or the climatic conditions, general or localized, may have made survival impossible.

Hundreds of the fossilized bones were removed by parties from the Carnegie Museum, the National Museum of Washington, D.C., and the University of Utah. These were not found as complete skeletons, but were disarticulated and widely scattered, although the major portion of them has been reassembled at various museums. A total of 26 nearly

91

complete skeletons, including 13 species who varied in weight from a few pounds to perhaps forty tons, plus many others partially incomplete, have been reconstructed. Since 1953 a few men have been constantly engaged in cleaning away the matrix of hard sandstone which surrounds the remaining fossils to provide deep-relief observation by the visitor, but further removals are not contemplated.

Fortunately, the steeply tilted strata are in such a position as to allow the dipping slope to form a northern wall of the building which was constructed at Visitor Center, thus presenting the fossils in place as upon an easel for the view of observers along the parallel balcony. Other rooms are used for preparation of fossil material, with windows provided for the public interest and curiosity.

Paleontologist Dr. Theodore E. White reliefing dinosaur bones. exposed in tilted beds of the Jurassic Morrison formation. (National Park Service)

Dinosaur Types

For the lover of long Latin names, let it be said that both orders of dinosaurs have been discovered here. One type has a bird-like pelvis, the *Ornithischia*, while others have a reptile-like pelvis, the *Saurischia.* The former were all vegetarian, but subdivisions of the latter were either vegetarian or meat-eaters. Two-footed types of the *Ornithischia* are the *Camptosaurus*, the *Dryosaurus*, and the *Laosaurus*, which grew to respective lengths of 17 feet to 2½ feet. The only four-footed type found here is the *Stegosaurus*, well known because of the bony plates in a double row along its back, also being a plant-eater.

Among the *Saurischia*, the genus *Antrodemus* represents the flesh-eating type, standing on its hind legs, and being about the size of a horse. Plant-eating types include *Apatosaurus*, about 70 feet long with a weight of about 40 tons, the long, slender *Diplodocus* with its whiplash tail, the

Mass of fossil bones in relief, including both vegetarian and carnivorous types of dinosaurs.

(From color slide by National Park Service)

long-necked *Barosaurus*, and two sizes of the genus *Camara-saurus*. National Park Service pamphlets describe all these forms in much more detail.

Besides the dinosaurs, only two other reptilian groups have been discovered at the Dinosaur National Monument quarry. There are two types of crocodiles, the larger being about the size of modern alligators, and the smaller being less than one foot long. Three species of turtles, much like today's pond turtles, are also known.

Canyon Country

The richly scenic canyon country of the Yampa and Green Rivers in Colorado, also extending into the eastern end of Utah's Uinta Mountains, was added to Dinosaur National Monument in 1938 rather than being descriptively and individually named in its own right.

The geology of the canyons is spectacular, but not geologically unusual. Strata formed under varying conditions during Paleozoic and early Mesozoic time resulted in a surficial flood plain of soft material into which the Yampa and Green Rivers cut their wide meandering curves. Uplift of the Colorado Plateau increased their erosive force, so that the curves became entrenched deeply through the red beds of much older sediments.

Goosenecks of the Yampa River in Colorado. (Compare these with the Goosenecks of the San Juan River in Utah.)

(From color slide from Ward's Nat. Sci. Est.)

94

COLORADO

BLACK CANYON OF THE GUNNISON National Monument
(Erosion)

This 22-square mile area in western Colorado was designated as a National Monument in 1933 to enclose the exceptional ten-mile portion of the gorge of the Gunnison River northeast of Montrose. The name derives both from the shadowed depths of the canyon, and from the geologic circumstance that it cuts through walls composed of dark, crystalline Precambrian rocks, similar to those within the lowest parts of the Grand Canyon of the Colorado River in Arizona.

The strata at the rim of the canyon are the common Mesozoic red sandstones and shales of the southwest, hundreds of millions of years younger in age.

View of the Black Canyon of the Gunnison River from Pioneer Point, northwest of the National Monument Boundary. (National Park Service)

Indeed, it may be difficult for the visitor to realize that the gap of missing strata between those of the gorge and of the rim corresponds approximately to the necessary time for life to evolve from one-celled types to the dinosaurs and most primitive mammals.

The Gunnison River, formed by junction of its tributaries which head westward of the crest of the continental divide, has been cutting downward for many million years through these extremely dense rocks, creating a canyon of much greater depth than width. The gorge, in fact, varies from about 1700 feet to 2400 feet deep, yet the rims are only 1300 feet apart where the canyon is most narrow.

Pioneer Point, from which the photo was taken, is actually not within the boundary of the national monument, but on the north rim of Black Canyon within the Curecanti Recreation area.

The north rim drive is reached from Delta, Colorado, and the south rim is accessible from Montrose.

COLORADO National Monument (Erosion)

Southwest of the ranchlands along the Colorado River valley in the western part of the state is the Uncompahgre Highland, about 4 miles west of Grand Junction and almost the same distance south of Fruita, just off U.S. 50.

Here is a great mass of red Mesozoic strata overlying dark crystalline rocks of Precambrian age. These consist of granite, gneiss, schist, and pegmatite dikes, forming the core of the Uncompahgre Highland. A tremendous time gap is represented by this great unconformity.

Paleozoic strata, if ever present, have been eroded away, and deposits of streams, lakes, and wind-blown sands probably occupied the surface at intervals. Then came the Laramide or Rocky Mountain uplift, about 100 million years ago, which elevated the region above the area sur-

Independence Monument — an erosional remnant of monolith, visible from Rim Rock Drive. (National Park Service)

rounding it. The Grand Mesa, toward the eastward, was covered by lava flows of less than a million years ago, during the Glacial Epoch.

Erosion, as always, began developing canyons in the surface. Continued faulting and jointing aided this, as for example, the 10-mile escarpment of red Cretaceous sandstone extending across the monument, now called Rim Rock Drive. Other portions of the region show fantastic towering monoliths, vividly colored layers in rampart walls, open caves, and fluted columns.

Independence Monument is a tall and narrow monolith visible from Rim Rock Drive, but reached only by hiking almost two miles along the Monument Canyon trail which begins at Trail Head considerably farther south.

A few of the other scenic spots along Rim Rock Drive which extends from northwest to southeast through the monument are Balanced Rock, Kissing Couple, Coke Ovens, and Liberty Cap. The last named requires a much longer hike than do the others.

Major canyons in the region are Red, Ute, Monument, and No Thoroughfare Canyons.

FLORISSANT FOSSIL BEDS National Monument
(Paleontology)

Florissant Fossil Beds is among the latest of National Park Service acquisitions, having been authorized in late 1969. At the present time of writing (1972) public access and physical development of the monument are still limited. An information station for visitors is available two miles south of the town of Florissant, Colorado, on Teller County Road #1.

The fossil beds are noted especially for the delicate preservation of fragile insects, tree foliage, and other forms of life.

The lake bed containing the strata is a curving outline about 12 miles long and 2 miles wide. It was formed during the Oligocene Epoch, about 34-35 million years ago, when a basaltic lava flow about 7 miles south of the town of Florissant blocked a meandering stream with 40-60 feet of mud. During intermittent volcanic activity continuing for the next 4 million years, ash and dust exploded into the air, finally settling into the lake, layer by layer. Life of the lakebed was probably about ½-million years. Leaves from the trees, with insects feeding on them, flying in the air, or settling on the water, were trapped in the volcanic ash.

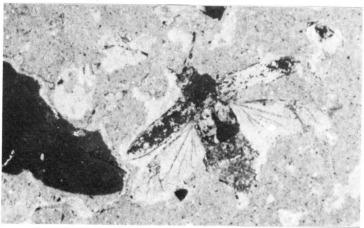

Fossil insect remains — preserved in volcanic ash. Fossil leaf appears at the left. (From color slide by National Park Service)

That which had fallen on land nearby was also washed into the lake by rains. These ashes slowly displaced the water, and a final lava flow sealed over the deposits.

These same Oligocene ash deposits also formed the famous John Day beds of central Oregon, containing an important assemblage of fossil mammals, plus many other types of animal and plant life. The excellent fish skeletons of Wyoming's Green River shale occur in similar fashion.

Also found at Florissant are stumps, wood, and leaves of willow, oak, maple, walnut, and pine, as well as more notable stumps of the *Sequoia*, comparable to California's living giant trees. The illustration shows what is thought to be the world's largest petrified stump, a *Sequoia* 74 feet in circumference, 14 feet high, and perhaps 34-40 million years old. Others are found in adjacent areas.

Petrified *Sequoia* Stump — believed to be the largest in the world. It is 38½ feet in circumference approximately 4 feet above base, and stands 11 feet high. (From color slide by National Park Service)

GREAT SAND DUNES National Monument
(Erosion and Deposition)

Between the Sangre de Cristo Mountains on the northeast and the San Juan Mountains to the west lies Colorado's San Luis Valley, location of the highest inland dunes in the United States. The San Luis Hills extend likewise to the southward, from which direction blow the prevailing winds. Alamosa is the nearest city, 38 miles in that direction. The general area is in the heart of the Rockies, east of the Continental Divide.

Geologic History

The San Luis Valley is geologically described as a graben, i.e., a fault-dropped wedge between two ranges. Its floor is from 7500 to 8000 feet above sea level. Subsequent to the existence of the inland sea which once extended from the Gulf of Mexico to the Arctic Ocean, generally coincident with the location of the present Rocky Mountains, crustal pressures caused the uplift of the region, compacting the accumulated sediments into hardened strata, and buckling these into high mountain crests, often accompanied by volcanic activity.

View of one of the many great sand dunes in the National Monument of that name, formed by both wind and water activity. (National Park Service)

Opinion is divided as to the origin of the tremendous amount of material forming the Great Sand Dunes. Some geologists believe that the light sandy soil of the San Luis Valley is transported across by the southwestern winds which rise as they cross the Sangre de Cristo Mountains. Under lowered velocity, they become forced to drop their load of sand over a ten-mile strip against the western base of this range. Other authorities consider that most of the sand was brought into the valley by streams from the mountains to the northeast, such as Medano Creek. Both sources undoubtedly are important.

The sand dunes themselves apparently have changed but little in general pattern during the hundreds of thousands of years since they began to form. All types, such as barchans, seifs, transverse, or longitudinal forms can be seen under varying conditions. Local shapes, however, may be noted as differing in details of appearance after each storm, especially when winds occur from the northeast, causing backward tilting of the dune crests. Strong southwestern winds restore the normal shape, with the sand visibly flowing over the gentle windward slope and down the steeper lee slope.

Medano Creek flows along the eastern boundary of the dune area, but finally disappears beneath the sand. Some of the smaller dunes to the eastward evidence their horizontal migration as they leave behind them skeletal trees, barren of branches and dead.

These dunes are undoubtedly the highest inland ones within the United States, accumulating to heights of at least 600 feet, according to the National Park Service, with some authorities ascribing heights of 800 or almost 1000 feet to the largest ones. The material is a brownish-gray silica, loose enough to entrap automobiles which have been foolishly driven off the main road to the headquarters and campground east of Medano Creek.

MESA VERDE National Park (Archeology, Diastrophism)

(Archeology is, of course, a branch of Anthropology, a science far afield from Geology. However, since Mesa Verde is the only archeological area yet given park status, it is also included here with emphasis upon its geologic data. A great many National Park Service monuments are strictly archeological, so have no place within the scope of this volume.)

Located in the extreme southwestern corner of Colorado, between the cities of Durango and Cortez, the Mesa Verde (Spanish for "green table") once supported a population of hundreds of people during various stages of their cultural development.

The earliest Basket Makers first lived in canyons near the mesa for several hundred years (0 to about 450 A.D.) in the fore part of the Christian era. They were farmers, knowing nothing of pottery, houses, or the bow and arrow. Their descendants, the Modified Basket Makers, left the first archeological remains on the mesa itself, occupying it until 750 A.D. They first lived in pithouses, but later built houses out in the open.

The Developmental Pueblo people lived on until 1100 A.D., with houses grouped together in villages, and made of many materials: adobe, sometimes combined with poles, stone slabs, and at last true masonry.

The climax of the Mesa Verde culture was reached between 1100 and 1300 A.D., known as the Great or Classic Pueblo Period. Pottery was characterized by more intricate, colored designs, hunting tools were devised, and kivas were built for religious or ceremonial rooms.

Repeated droughts began in the latter part of the century, the longest having been determined by tree rings as from 1276 to 1289 A.D. Springs dried up, and the people became compelled to leave their villages to find more dependable water supplies. They drifted southward into the Rio Grande area of New Mexico or the Hopi Country in Arizona, where many of the Pueblo Indians there today may be descended from their Mesa Verde ancestors. The mesa was abandoned before 1300, long before the arrival of the Spanish in the latter 1700's.

Geologically, the mesa is essentially of the Mesaverde formation of the Mesozoic Upper Cretaceous Period. The lowest unit in the park is the Mancos shale, dark gray to black in color, and of marine origin. It was formed in the shallow sea which extended from the Arctic to the Gulf of Mexico, as heretofore mentioned. As the sea retreated, coarse land sediments filled the basin, forming the Mesaverde formation. Lowest of these is the Point Lookout sandstone, which forms the cliffs facing the highway. Above this is the Menefee coal, with some shale. Uppermost is the Cliff House sandstone, the dark yellowish cliff-forming sandstone which easily weathered into caves in which the Indians built their cliff houses.

The mesa is a large fault block which was uplifted in the late Cretaceous or early Tertiary time. After leaving Cortez (elevation 6198 feet) along U.S. 160 and driving about 10 miles along the valley to the park entrance, one climbs a few miles of switchbacks to some 1500 feet higher at the top of the mesa. The remainder of the 21 miles to the Park Headquarters and main ruins, still several miles from the south rim, passes over a gently sloping highway, seemingly of no significant drop in elevation. The visitor is therefore astounded when a ranger at headquarters tells him that he is now back to an elevation comparable with that at the entrance before he so carefully conquered the twists and turns in that upward climb. Even so, the south rim is still high above the arid plains of northwestern New Mexico, with the volcanic plug of Shiprock dimly visible in the distance.

Streams and weathering have produced more than 20 large dendritic canyons tributary to the Mancos River, all more or less parallel and sloping southward across the mesa. Within the top layer of buff-yellow sandstone along the upper walls of the canyons are wind-scoured caves within which the cliff-dwellers built and occupied apartment-like homes during the last one hundred years of mesa occupation. While many visitors think of these cliff-houses as typical of Mesa Verde, they really represent only a small fragment of the time when the early Indians lived in their pit houses and pueblos on top of the mesa.

Cliff Palace, the largest such in the southwest, is in a cave 500 feet long and 100 feet deep. It, together with Spruce Tree House and Square Tower House, was discovered by cowboys Richard Wetherill and Charles Mason in 1888.

Cliff Palace contains more than 223 rooms and kivas; Spruce Tree House held 114 rooms, and probably accommodated between 200 and 250 people. Spruce Tree House is the only one open to the public on a year-around basis, visited by a self guiding tour with a ranger in charge at the house itself.

Most excavations in the park have been done by the Smithsonian Institution, the Park Service, and the University of Colorado since 1909 with some subsidiary studies by the National Geographic Society.

Cliff Palace, the largest such prehistoric dwelling in the southwest. It contains more than 223 rooms and kivas. (National Park Service)

ROCKY MOUNTAIN National Park   (Igneous Intrusive, Glaciation)

Rocky Mountain National Park, northwest of Denver and Boulder, presents a complex geological history, yet is typical of the general nature of the Rockies. The Front Range is essentially the batholithic granite of the Mesozoic era, highly folded and faulted. The foothills eastward are Cretaceous sediments, sometimes containing dinosaur remains and associated fossils.

The ancestral range was uplifted and folded from the trough in the sea floor where thousands of feet of sediments had been laid. Rock fracturing and faulting occurred, allowing intrusive granites and extrusive lavas to accumulate. Erosion of this highland exposed these crystalline cores of the range as it wore down to a rolling topography. The gentle slopes of Trail Ridge and similar areas indicate the last stages of this erosion. Some eruptions of volcanoes along the western portion were followed by further erosion.

View of the Rocky Mountains from Trail Ridge Road, which is east of the Continental Divide. Closed during part of the winter.

(From color slide from Ward's Nat. Sci. Est.)

106

Trail Ridge Road follows an old Indian trail, well known to mountain-lovers throughout the country. It is a broad, seasonal road on the eastern side of the Continental Divide from near Fall River Pass, at an elevation of 11,796 feet, past the highest point on the road, at 12,183 feet, thence toward the southeast via Many Parks Curve and on toward the Park Headquarters which also serves Estes Park. From Fall River Pass southwestward across the divide, and then south to Timber Creek, the 25 miles between there and Many Parks Curve is closed during winter months. Southward from Timber Creek the road continues to Grand Lake, another entrance, and still another entry point is in the southeast corner.

From Trail Ridge Road one can see many of the 107 named peaks in the park which are more than 11,000 feet in elevation. Of these, Longs Peak rises to 14,256 feet in the southeastern park area. Formerly considered impossible to climb, a cable route now assists climbers upward.

In the Pleistocene Epoch about two million years ago, as through all the northwestern and northern states, glaciers of the Ice Age were formed. Mountain glaciers of the high ranges carved out U-shaped valleys and cirques, with morainal materials being deposited below the fronts of the glaciers. A few small glaciers still remain in the highest valleys. Moraine Park contains good examples of glacial deposits.

HAWAII

HALEAKALA National Park (Volcanism)

Haleakala Volcano forms the eastern half of the island of Maui. Its summit, consisting of less than an eighth of the total area of the volcano, was designated as a separate national park in 1961, as distinct from Hawaii Volcanoes National Park.

An interesting legend refers to the name of this volcano, which is one of the most picturesque in Hawaii. Its translated meaning is "House of the Sun," based on an old island tale which relates that once a Polynesian god named Maui climbed to the mountain top to hold back the sun's movement through the sky so that his mother would have more hours of daylight for completion of her daily tasks.

Geologic History

Beginning as a typical shield volcano about 20 million years ago, like Mauna Loa, Kilauea, and others of the Hawaiian group, a vast number of thin flows built up Haleakala to an elevation of more than 11,000 feet, reduced now by erosion to 10,023 feet. Two deep valleys which joined into a long transverse trough were eroded during this time of volcanic inactivity.

Resumption of eruptions near the margins of the cone and within this depression almost entirely filled the valleys, while the ash, cinders, and pumice expelled along the diagonal fissures created a series of symmetrical cones on this line. The time of this eruptive action has not yet been determined, but in the late 1700's a flow occurred near the ocean on the southwest side of the crater.

The volcano has been dormant since then, although earthquake tremors have sometimes been noted which indicate that it may not yet be quite extinct.

This view from the western rim of the main crater shows very well the secondary cones developed along the fault zone.

Haleakala Crater, Maui, from the west rim. Note line of cones from subsequent eruptions along fissures. (National Park Service)

Hard surfaced roads do surround the island of Maui, but none lead into the crater. Several trails for hiking or horseback riding are available, but visitors are warned that it is a strenuous trip for one day because of the high elevation. Those planning to enter the crater are required to register in advance with the park ranger. Several shorter trail trips are also available.

HAWAII VOLCANOES National Park (Volcanism)

Hawaii Volcanoes National Park, on the island of Hawaii, includes some of the world's largest and most active volcanoes. Especially interesting is the fact that they are so safely accessible to visitors even during eruptions, which are usually of the quiet type, in contrast to those more explosive.

The Hawaiian Islands are actually the tops of a magnificent mountain range rising up from the floor of the Pacific Ocean. Mauna Kea and Mauna Loa are the largest volcanoes and mountain masses on earth, with bases at least 15,000 feet below sea level, and elevations of about 13,700 feet above sea level. Thus they are at least as high as Everest and much more bulky, considering total dimensions.

Volcanic Activity

Long ago at some indeterminate time in geologic history, a fracture opened from northwest to southeast across part of the ocean floor. Volcanic materials gradually accumulated from below the crust, finally rising into great peaks forming islands such as Hawaii, Oahu, and six other major ones, constituting the Hawaiian Range. The oldest rocks which are exposed above sea level are probably late Tertiary in age, dating back 10 to 25 million years ago.

The youngest of these islands, also the largest and southernmost, is Hawaii. At the tip of the north end of the island is the oldest of its five volcanoes, Kohala, now long extinct and deeply eroded. Mauna Kea, next to the southward, last erupted some 15,000 years ago, after glaciation of its summit. Hualalai, on the western coast, erupted in 1801, but not again. The two southern volcanoes, Mauna Loa and Kilauea, are still vigorously active.

These are typical of the quiet, shield type of volcano, in which the lava is very fluid, and so flows quietly down the slopes. Such flows produce the ropy "pahoehoe" lava, in contrast to the explosive "aa" type. The profile of such volcanoes is therefore low; the slope of Mauna Loa varies from 2° at the base to only 12° at the summit, whereas the slopes of cinder cones may be 30° to 40°.

As the peaks rise above the ocean surface, erosional action begins. Canyons and cliffs develop, while platforms of eroded material form across the cones at shallow sub-surface levels. Incidentally, to the west of the Hawaiian Islands is the Leeward Group of fourteen or more basaltic platforms, of which five are below water level.

Eruptions from Mauna Loa have been recorded since 1832, averaging one per 3½ years. They usually begin near the summit, then move to fissures along the flanks, with quiet flows to seaward. The 1950 eruption was the greatest since 1859, with perhaps a billion tons of lava spewed out by six major flows at a maximum speed of 10 miles per hour.

Kilauea has been formed to the eastward of Mauna Loa, and is surrounded by more explosive debris of two types. One is glassy fragments from lava fountains; the second is mostly stony material from previous flows as thrown outward by steam explosions, as in 1924. Its most distinctive feature is the Fire Pit, known as Halemaumau, definitely connected with the underground source of the lava. The surface temperature was about 1750°F., with the depth varying greatly, sometimes sinking from view, then pouring over the edges.

Eruption of Halemaumau Crater, Kileauea, on Hawaii. Its Fire Pit is believed to be connected with the underground lava source.

This existed during much of the 19th century, and until 1924, when the walls caved in and ground water entered the tube. This resulted in many violent steam explosions, and expulsion of fragmentary portions of the older side wall material.

After a period of relative quiet between 1934 and 1952, a series of lava fountains and flows developed along an eastern fissure. In 1954 the fountains reached a maximum height of 600 feet. In early 1955 flows of "pahoehoe" and "aa" lava spread gradually, with three at last reaching the ocean coast. Scientists now for the first time were able to study the sequence of volcanic vent formation closely, from barely visible cracks to increasing expulsions of lava and gas, terminating in flows and fountains.

During October and November of 1959 an increasing number of earthquakes began at Kilauea, finally resulting in cracking the wall of Kilauea Iki, a small adjacent pit crater. A line of fountains began pouring lava into the main crater, burying the old 1968 floor. All but one soon ceased, but intermittent eruptions continued here until the maximum height which was ever recorded, 1900 feet, was reached. Cinders built a conical hill on the crater rim, pumice covered the surface half a mile away, and a pool of lava 380 feet deep remained in the lake afterward, when the eruption ended on December 21. However it was less than a month before the eruptions began again.

In January and February, 1960, further fountains of lava formed along the eastern line of faulting. The flows destroyed most of Kapoho village, but on reaching the sea they created about 500 acres of new land. The top of Kilauea subsided and Halemaumau's floor collapsed, forming a basin 150 feet deep, within which three deeper pits developed. Only minor activity has been recorded since 1961.

CALIFORNIA

DEATH VALLEY National Monument   (Diastrophism)

Death Valley, located mainly in California, adjacent to Nevada and east of Owens Lake, has been described as the most desolate region in the United States. During the days of the California gold rush, although only one man actually died of thirst within Death Valley, many others perished of hunger or thirst along the adjacent trails. Plants exist throughout the aridity and heat of summer by modifications of their leaves or root systems. Animal life is fairly common, although most of them travel and feed at night. Birds are well known, some living on the valley floor permanently, others making their homes in the nearby mountains, while still others are merely migratory. The central salt flats, however, have neither plant nor animal life.

Therefore when Death Valley was approved as a National Monument, opposition was widely expressed against popularizing this valley of poisonous water, bleached bones, drifting sand, and salt flats as a natural exhibit. "Who would go there?" — "Too dangerous!" — "Uninteresting!" — "Not scenic!" — exclaimed critics. Nevertheless, it now ranks as a popular place for visitors, exceeded in size only by Katmai National Monument and Yellowstone and Mount McKinley National Parks, and averaging 15,000 sight-seers monthly, including the hottest summer season of June throughout September when temperatures may climb to as much as 134°F. Some describe the months of November to April as having an ideal climate.

Geologically, Death Valley contains an almost complete record of time and processes. All eras and most of the periods are included in the strata, and volcanism, sedimentation, metamorphism, and diastrophism have all been active.

The valley is a down-faulted block between two mountain uplifts. It is about 135 miles long and 4 to 16 miles wide, between the Panamint and Amargosa Ranges, and 500 square miles are below sea level. Bad Water is the lowest dry land spot in the Western Hemisphere, officially surveyed at −282 feet elevation.

Bad Water, the lowest point in Death Valley, at an elevation of -282 feet (below sea level!). (National Park Service)

The eastern side of the Sierra Nevada is a major fault scarp, including Mount Whitney towering over Owens River Valley at 14,495 feet, the highest elevation in the 48 states.

The mountains are mainly of Mesozoic granite, from which much quartz sand has been produced by weathering, becoming material of which the sand dunes are formed. The complex history of Death Valley has only partly been untangled. During the Ice Age several lakes existed in the valley, of which the largest was Lake Manly, about 90 miles long and 600 feet deep, according to its ancient shore lines still visible along the mountain sides. With the change of these fresh water lakes into playas, alkaline materials such as borax were deposited. Crystalline salt pinnacles and gravels also formed, seen in the Devils Golf Course, south of Furnace Creek Ranch.

Even though annual precipitation is now less than 2 inches, water-worn phenomena can be seen. North of Bad

114

Water is Natural Bridge, and farther up the canyon is evidence of an extinct waterfall once 20 feet wide. Nature can be amazingly contradictory!

Among other areas of particular interest is the Borax Museum, located at Park Village in the Furnace Creek oasis, which depicts the story of borax mining. Here the phrase "20-Mule Team Borax" originated. It is supervised by the U. S. Borax and Chemical Corporation.

Dantes View is 60 miles from Park Village. There are several short side roads en route, and a last 12 miles of climbing. From here one has a marvelous view of the valley, almost 6000 feet below, and extending north and south. Bad Water is directly below, and toward the west Telescope Peak, still a mile higher at 11,049 feet.

There is a cross route including Eastside and Westside Roads, between Rhyolite, Nevada, and Panamint Springs, California, thence on to Lone Pine where a good view of Mount Whitney can be seen.

The northern section of the park contains Ubehebe Crater, an 800-foot deep volcanic pit caused by a violent volcanic explosion. This is only a short distance from Scotty's Castle, from which a road leads to Bonnie Claire, Nevada.

Scotty's Castle is near the northern boundary. Originally reputed to have been constructed by the prospector's gold discoveries, it was later revealed to have been built for Death Valley Scotty by his Chicago millionaire friend, A. M. Johnson. Scotty's grave is located nearby.

DEVILS POSTPILE National Monument (Volcanism)

Here, as in so many other places, the poor old Devil receives the blame for another of Nature's oddities, located 13 miles airline southeast of Yosemite National Park. A lava flow of about 900,000 years ago spread six miles through the canyon of the middle fork of the San Joaquin River near the summit of the Sierra Nevada, forming a colonnade 900 feet in length and 200 feet high composed of basaltic columns.

Columnar Posts — usually five or six-sided, due to contractional cooling forming joints at 120° angles.
(National Park Service)

Their regularity of shape and size, individually being 40-60 feet high, and the abundance of typical five or six sided shapes suggest almost ideal conditions for such a formation to have been created.

The central portion of lava flows is likely to lose its heat in twenty years or less, primarily to the adjacent walls or the floor of the extrusion. Since these exterior portions cannot possibly shrink uniformly toward the center, tensions develop. Shrinkage occurs around equally spaced centers, resulting in short cracks connecting these, usually in sets of three at 120° interior angles, and thus producing hexagonal columns under ideal conditions. Irregularities may be present, as with thermal conductivity, causing columns to be five or seven sided, or incomplete, or changes in vertical curvature may appear.

The area has been glaciated, producing two effects worth mentioning. One side of the Postpile was cut away by the ice, exposing a wall of columns in unusual detail. The upper surface was also eroded horizontally smooth, presenting a mosaic appearance of sections.

Bubbling hot springs hereabouts indicate continuance of subsurface heat. Pumice has been found in the northern portion of the monument, probably wind-blown from Mono Crater.

(LA BREA PITS - Paleontology)

The famous tar pits of Rancho La Brea, while not under the National Park Service, but being locally supervised by the Los Angeles County Museum at Hancock Park, do constitute a unique paleontological phenomenon. There are two similar, but smaller, occurrences of tar pit fossilization in California, one in Kern County, the other in Santa Barbara County. ("La Brea" is the Spanish translation of "tar.")

The first record of these tar seeps was made by Gaspar de Portola in his account of his 1769 California Expedition. In 1972 Jose Martinez reported that these liquid petroleum or asphalt springs had been observed to entrap small animals and birds, and that he had collected several bone specimens which had risen to the top after years of burial. Mining of asphalt on the ranch then owned by Major Henry Hancock initiated a report on the bones found therein as described by William Denton, who was given a canine tooth of a sabretooth cat, and collected other bird and mammalian bones.

Tar pit at Hancock Park, Los Angeles County Museum, California, from which the bones of many prehistoric animals have been excavated.

Scientific explorations by the University of California and other scientific institutions by permission of Madame Ida Hancock Ross and Mr. G. Allan Hancock were continued between 1906 and 1915, and the Hancock collection was established by the Los Angeles County Museum as a memorial to them. In 1915 Mr. Hancock deeded the 23-acre tract to Los Angeles County for the exhibition and preservation of its scientific discoveries, and Hancock Park was thus developed on Wilshire Boulevard.

Many asphalt pits are scattered within the park, some containing fresh tar with gas bubbles surfacing, others being more or less dry. Observation Pit is in the western portion, protected by a roofed building. A circular staircase leads to a lower platform which allows one to view various bones in the original positions within the tar bed below.

It must be emphasized that some of the open pits may be as they existed during Pleistocene time, but many others are the result of excavations during the last 40 years. Studies of the fossil remains definitely place them as existent during the very last Glacial Epoch.

The asphalt beds are part of a series of sedimentary gravels, sands, and clays, all underlain by marine oil sands. Most of the fossil bones were found within the upper 20 feet of strata, with 30-40 feet as maximum depth. Excavations were barricaded at the sides as digging proceeded to avoid danger of cave-in.

The Los Angeles County Museum booklet, "Rancho La Brea," lists these animals as among those discovered: bears, wolves, cats (including the sabre-tooth tiger), rodents, rabbits, horses, camels, deer, bison, mastodons, elephants and ground sloths. Modern birds, also snakes, lizards, toads, and frogs are known. A few invertebrates, especially insects, have been found. One human skull, a few bone fragments, and several artifacts such as atlatl dart foreshafts were discovered amid the more ancient diggings. (The "atlatl" was a prehistoric device using a notched stick to hurl a dart over a greater distance.) These humans may or may not have been contemporaneous with extinct animals found among the fauna.

LASSEN VOLCANIC National Park (Volcanism)

Lassen Peak is notable as the only recently active volcano within the United States, exclusive of Alaska and Hawaii. It is the most southerly of the volcanic cones of the Cascade Range, located in northern California about 50 miles east of Redding. Like Mount Rainier and the others, it is of composite type, formed by quiet lava flows mixed with cinders and ash, probably once at least 14,000 feet high and 15 miles in diameter.

Lassen Peak, showing mud flow and avalanche area from the western side. (From color slide from Ward's Nat. Sci. Est.)

Volcanic Activity

Its parent peak was apparently Mount Tehama, another giant cone formed during the Miocene Epoch about 25 million years ago when volcanic activity was intense all along the entire Pacific Coast.

Near the end of the last Ice Age, a time about 10,000 years ago, Lassen Peak was formed as a plug volcano 3 miles out upon the north slope of Tehama, when a stiff mass of lava, too viscous to flow, was pushed upward to create a 2,500-foot steeply sided dome. A portion of this can be seen on Lassen's southern slope, but most of it is buried beneath talus. Similar plug intrusions formed Chaos Crags, Eagle Peak, and Bumpass Mountain on the flanks of Lassen's heights.

This expulsion of lava may have caused the collapse of the larger part of Tehama into the chamber below, according to one theory, comparable to the history of Mount Mazama in Oregon. Brokeoff Mountain is the largest remaining fragment of the old rim, others being Mount Diller, Mount Conard, and the lower part of Pilot Pinnacle. Several steam explosions occurred at the north base of the Crags, perhaps as early as 250 A.D., with others following in about 1250 A.D. and 1691 A.D. These caused three successive avalanches which produced the Chaos Jumbles, also damming Manzanita Creek to form the lovely lake of the same name.

Lassen itself had slept peacefully ever since the time of its original formation, with the symmetrical Cinder Cone and the Fantastic Lava Beds developing subsequently at the northeast portion of the park.

The Fremont Expedition of 1843 told of mild eruptions of Mount Baker and Mount St. Helens northward in Washington, which spread ashes over the region. During the winter of 1850-51 "flaring lights" were seen from a distance of 160 miles, presumably from Cinder Cone. In 1858 activity was reported in Mount Baker's crater, reddening the clouds above, while heated vapors arose from fumaroles on both Mount Rainier and Mount Shasta.

A hunter named Bumpass, according to legend, was showing to his friends his discovery of steam vents and mudpots on the south slopes of Lassen Peak in 1865, when he accidentally thrust his foot through the crust into the scalding mud below, exactly as he had been warning them not to do. Whatever his remarks may actually have been, the area now carries the name of "Bumpass Hell," and park service signs warn visitors against doing the very same thing today.

Suddenly, with no previous warnings by smoke vapors or earth tremors, Mount Lassen returned to life at 5:00 a.m., Memorial Day, May 30, 1914. The ranger on duty reported the spouting of lava, ash, dust, stones, and fine sand, with accompanying steam and other gases, although much of the material was cold. A new deeply fissured crater 44 feet long and 25 feet wide opened near the top of the peak. Activity continued, but only irregularly during that summer and fall. The winter of 1914-15 was marked by a heavy snowfall, which may have contributed to the next major eruption as the extra water penetrated the mountain, thus increasing steam pressure within.

On the night of May 19, 1915, watchers saw a red line forming along the northeastern rim, which rapidly expanded as molten lava began to spill over and pour down the side of the peak for 1000 feet or so. The ensuing rapidity with which the snow melted caused a torrential mud flow into Hat and Lost Creek valleys, with uprooted trees, debris, and large rocks being carried down the slope. One of these is said to have remained warm to the touch for a week afterward, and is labelled "Hot Rock" where it lies close to the highway at present.

The climax came three days later, on the afternoon of May 22, when an explosion of terrific force shot horizontally out from the northeast face of the mountain, hurling a cloud of smoke which rose 5 miles into the air. The violence of the eruption destroyed all small life in its path and knocked down belts of the forested area in the direction of the mud flow for a distance of 3 miles. This fan-shaped region now is called "The Devastated Area."

Lassen's internal energy was largely expended in these explosions, although there were eight more minor eruptions during June and six after that in July. By 1917 all major activity had apparently subsided, except for a few fumaroles issuing steam and other gases near Lassen's summit. A total of 289 bursts were recorded between 1914 and 1921.

At present Lassen must be classed as a dormant volcano, in contrast to others in the Cascade Range which seem to be approaching extinction. Visitors often inquire when the next eruption may occur. The only true answer must be "We don't know," although some volcanists have suggested this as a possibility during the next decade.

Lassen Peak, viewed from the southwest. Last eruptions were in 1914 - 1915, the last occurrence of such within the 48 states.

(National Park Service)

LAVA BEDS National Monument (Volcanism)

(Although actually in California, Lava Beds is grouped with the Pacific Northwest by the National Park Service for administrative geographical convenience.)

Near Tulelake, California, only a few miles from the state's northern boundary, lies the rugged landscape of Lava Beds. All types of extrusive volcanism are well displayed here. The southern part of the monument contains the majority of the 17 cinder cones, while flows of lava show both the rough "aa" and the ropy "pahoehoe" forms. Three of the largest fields are the Schonchin, Black Lava, and Devil's Homestead flows, of which the last named is most recent, probably less than 1000 years old. The earlier flows and cones, however, date back to Miocene volcanic activity.

Chimneys, tunnels or tubes, and caves are notable features of the basaltic display. Almost 300 lava tubes are now known, with more probably undiscovered; of these about 190 have been explored to some extent, but only 18 are open to the public at present.

Such tubes and caves formed when the lava surface cooled, and the lower liquid portions flowed on, leaving chambers behind. A few caves contain "lava-cicles," formed by the splashing of liquid material up to the ceiling, or by remelting of parts of the ceiling by the hot gases escaping from the molten rock beneath.

Many of the caves, such as Merrill and Skull Ice Caves, contain ice throughout every year, due to trapping of the more dense, cold winter air below which then freezes ground water entering the grotto. Skulls of bighorn sheep have been found in the upper of three levels in Skull Cave, the lowest being solid ice.

Petroglyphs and colored pictures are found on walls of cliffs and caves, drawn by prehistoric tribes, long before Modoc Indians sought refuge there during their war in 1872-73.

Ridge formed from blocks of basaltic lava, mostly erupted within the
last 1000 years. (National Park Service)

PINNACLES National Monument   (Volcanism, Diastrophism)

This area of volcanic and earthquake activity lies primarily in San Benito County, with a small southwestern corner in Monterey County, and comprises a part of the Gabilan Range. It is located southeast of Salinas, on U.S. 101, and adjacent to Soledad.

At the beginning of the Cenozoic Era, California had been eroded to become a wide stretch of nearly flat land. Thin gravels covered the vastly older granitic bedrock. During mid-Miocene time, about 23.5 million years ago according to potassium-argon dating, mountain building pressures forced the granite masses upward, and liquid magma from below began to intrude through the faulted cracks, then to spread over the surface. This was not the dark basalt of many lava flows, but mainly consisted of rhyolite, the finely crystalline equivalent of granite, likewise of light color. More abundant than flows, however, were the explosive eruptions which showered the region with many tons of sharp-edged rock fragments, later to be cemented into a breccia by percolation of mineral-bearing ground water.

A major fissure which was active in extruding the flow extended in a north-south direction. Here, during later activity, the lava became very viscous, plugging most of the fissure. Five remaining vents, characterized by vertically banded rhyolite and volcanic tuff, developed between South Chalone Peak and the Visitor Center area. These gradually merged into one large, steep-sided, elongated volcano, from which further flows and explosive materials were scattered far and wide. This ancient volcano apparently once rose to an elevation of about 8,000 feet, nearly a mile higher than the monument's highest point, North Chalone Peak.

As the volcanic action ceased, there developed two large faults, likewise north-south in direction, one on each side of the monument. The central block dropped downward, geologically known as a graben, somewhat more rapidly on the eastern side, thus producing a tilt in that direction where erosion therefore took place more rapidly. The Chalone Creek fault is to the east, while the Pinnacles fault is at the western side. This angular tilting is easily seen by the visitor walking along the monument's trails. The famous San Andreas fault which caused the San Francisco earthquake of 1906, as well as current repeated shocks, is only 6 miles eastward of these, and may or may not have been related to them. Dropping of the central block may have been due to the withdrawal of the subsurface magma pool.

Further erosion and sliding of loose blocks from the volcanic rim, together with joint fractures which developed, form the 500-1200 foot spires and pinnacles seen today, particularly along the western flank, which then became further widened by weathering.

Machete Ridge, near the Old Pinnacles Campground and Trail, is one of the most spectacular formations.

Also notable are the "caves" which were formed by fault movements causing many blocks of rock to slide down into narrow canyons and become wedged between the valley walls, blocking off most of the daylight. Examples of such are found in Bear Gulch and Old Pinnacles "Caves."

Machete Ridge, of basaltic material, formed along the Old Pinnacles fault line. (National Park Service)

POINT REYES National Seashore (Diastrophism, Shorelines)

Point Reyes is the only one of the National Shorelines of geologic interest to be included in this volume.

The Point Reyes Peninsula, about 35 miles northwest of San Francisco, is geologically separated from the mainland by the San Andreas fault, which created the depressions of Tomales and Bolinas Bays. Tomales Bay, the larger, extends northwestward, while Bolinas Bay is aligned with it toward the southeast. The intervening land area is traversed by the state highway No. 1, within the rift zone, while Sir Frances Drake Highway from San Rafael crosses it at Olema and continues across the area to the very tip of the peninsula.

Toward the west is the higher ground of Inverness Ridge, then a gently rolling portion with coastal marshes, and finally there is the Point Reyes Promontory itself.

Point Reyes Peninsula, curling around Drake's Bay, and ending in the promontory above the ocean.   (National Park Service)

The peninsula is currently being displaced toward the northwest along the fault line at the rate of about 2 inches per year, which has continued for the past 80 million years. The San Francisco earthquake of April 18, 1906 caused a side movement of about 20 feet at the head of Tomales Bay. Some geologists believe that formations on both sides of the fault may have been united about 150 million years ago.

Point Reyes itself is classed as an excellent example of a sea cliff with adjoining wave-built beaches. Wave and current action are constantly at work eroding away portions of the cliff and carrying the material elsewhere along the shore to produce these gently sloping beaches. Other features of marine geology are sea caves, offshore rocks, and a 3-mile sand spit. The semicircular south shoreline encloses Drake's Bay, with Drake's Estero as a marshy lagoon extending inland.

SEQUOIA and KINGS CANYON National Parks
(Diastrophism, Glaciation, Botany)

These two adjacent parks are about 70 miles southeast of Yosemite, which they much resemble in geologic history, rock formations, and presence of giant sequoia redwood trees. Kings Canyon is somewhat larger than its southward neighbor, with respective areas of 719 and 605 square miles.

Sequoia National Park was established in 1890, thus being our second oldest park, for the purpose of protecting the giant trees from the logging industry. The former General Grant National Park was also created in that same year, but in 1940 this small area was included within the new Kings Canyon National Park. Each park, nevertheless, has its own distinctive differences.

Geologic History

All three parks mentioned are parts of the western slope of the Sierra Nevada. This mountain range has been produced by three stages of folding, faulting, and uplift. The first of these ancestral ranges began toward the end of the Permian Period, more than 200 million years ago. Marine Paleozoic sediments were uplifted and folded out of their former sea-level position. Erosion again wore down these ranges to sea level, and further subsidence of the area brought it again under water, allowing deposition of early Mesozoic marine sediments and volcanic materials. A second uplift closing the Cretaceous Period, about 135 million years ago, again crumpled these into parallel folds in a northwesterly direction, into which great batholithic intrusions of granite forced their way during Jurassic time, crystallizing into solid rock containing disseminated amounts of what later became concentrated into California's placer gold. During the Cretaceous, erosion again cut away the sedimentary strata as well as much of the igneous material, leaving the Sierra region low and flat except for the hills extending northwestward.

Beginning with the Tertiary Period, four main uplifts and several lesser ones next raised the range as a series of fault blocks many thousand feet higher, with a corresponding depression of the eastern block now occupied by the Owens River Valley. Here we note the odd contrast between Mount

Whitney, the highest point within the contiguous 48 states (14,495 feet elevation), and Death Valley, about 80 miles eastward, whose lowest point at Bad Water is −282 feet, that is, below sea level.

Three distinct glacial intervals then followed in the Pleistocene Epoch forming typical features such as U-shaped valleys, cirques, moraines, erratics, and grooved surfaces. The granite domes are perhaps most distinctive, such as Moro Rock, North Dome, Tehipite Dome, and others, produced by exfoliation as was Yosemite's famous Half Dome.

Interestingly enough, while most of the Sierra is composed of granite, some limestone formations have been metamorphosed into marble, into which ground water seepage has cut caves in the usual way. Crystal Cave, to the west of Giant Forest in the southwestern part of Sequoia National Park, is the only one open to the public, although others are known.

The Redwoods

The redwoods must of course be included on a geo-botanical basis. Only three species exist of those which once were abundant over the world. The giants are the *Sequoia gigantea*, of which more than 70 groves occupy the western Sierra slopes.

The famous General Sherman tree in the Giant Forest has a diameter of 36.5 feet at its base, a circumference there of 101.6 feet, and a height of 272.4 feet to top of trunk. In addition to being the largest living thing on earth, it was formerly thought also to be the oldest, with an estimated age of 3500 - 4000 years. Authorities now believe the smaller bristle cone pine, a soft alpine Western type, to be older.

The coast redwood, *Sequoia sempervirens*, is still important in the lumber industry of California and Oregon. *Metasquoia*, or the "dawn redwood," formerly known only as a Miocene fossil form, was discovered in China in the 1940 - 50 decade by a native forester. Specimens were sent to China's National Central University, who invited Dr. Ralph W. Chaney, paleobotanist at the University of California, to study it. This redwood, unlike the Pacific coast types, sheds its needles annually.

Group of California's famous redwood trees, known as *Sequoia,* *gigantea*, the "giant" species; the lumber industry uses the species *Sequoia sempervirens.* (National Park Service)

King's Canyon

Kings Canyon National Park has been described as 99% wilderness, with the canyon area along the south fork of Kings River being the only developed portion. The canyon, 10 miles long and half a mile wide, has walls of from 2,500 to 6,000 feet in height, while the top of Spanish Mountain is nearly 8000 feet above the river.

The General Grant tree and other giant sequoias are located in the small area toward the west previously mentioned, now known as General Grant Grove. The General Grant tree has a circumference of 107.6 feet, which is six feet greater than the General Sherman tree, but it is five feet less in height.

Unlike Yosemite National Park, Kings Canyon has no high waterfalls, but it does contain the two next highest cliffs, Grand Sentinel at 3,500 feet, and Tehipite Dome, 3,200 feet above the river bed. Yosemite's El Capitan, in comparison, rises 3,562 feet above the valley floor.

Kings Canyon and Kings River in the southern portion of Kings Canyon National Park, otherwise largely wilderness area.

(From color slide from Ward's Nat. Sci. Est.)

133

YOSEMITE National Park
(Igneous Intrusive, Diastrophism, Stream Erosion, Glaciation)

Yosemite National Park is in east central California, on the western slopes of the Sierra Nevada, and was known to the Yosemite Indians as Ah-wah-nee ("deep grassy valley"). As indicated above, its magnificent scenery may be described as the combined result of several geologic processes: sedimentation, igneous intrusion, folding, faulting, stream erosion and glaciation.

The valley was first seen from some distance northward by a mountaineer, Joseph Reddeford Walker, in 1833. Major James D. Savage, leader of an expedition against the Indian inhabitants of the valley in 1851, is usually given credit for its discovery.

Sequoias are also well known in Yosemite National Park, particularly in the beautiful Mariposa Grove.

Geologic History

The geologic history of Yosemite Valley has been the subject of much controversy for many years, and numerous theories even yet disagree with each other in details, although it is now universally accepted that glaciation was the major factor in the modern scenery of the Park. Strikingly enough, however, even an early California state geologist is quoted as denying the presence of glaciers in any part of the valley at any time. Instead, he ascribed the origin of the area to a great cataclysm during which withdrawal of subsurface magmas resulted in its sinking deeply downward.

The great naturalist, John Muir, who followed the studies of Europe's famous glacial authority, Louis Agassiz, lived in the valley from 1868 to 1874. By 1870 he began serious exploration of the highlands and valleys in search of evidence which corroborated his belief that glaciation, aided by stream erosion, had been of primary importance in carving out Yosemite's cliffs, domes, canyons and waterfalls.

Dr. Francois E. Matthes, topographer and geologist for the U.S. Geological Survey, mapped the valley in 1905-6, and later wrote essays and a final professional paper in 1930 on the geological history of Yosemite Valley. Yet even now this is considered outdated by authorities, so rapidly do new theories progress.

Nevertheless, the following generalized summary of Yosemite's geology can safely be written. It has already been stated that the three Parks — Sequoia, Kings Canyon, and Yosemite — share the general origin of the Sierra Nevada as rapidly reviewed here.

Precambrian formations are not identifiable within the Park. Paleozoic shallow embayments spread over eastern California, also into Nevada and Utah, forming deposits of sand, mud, and lime which hardened into sandstone, shale, and limestone; these in turn became metamorphosed into quartzite, slate, schist, or marble, particularly during the mountain building of the Permian Period.

This action produced the first ancestral Sierra Nevada of the region. These oldest rocks known in Yosemite National Park are collectively identified as the Calaveras Formation, well shown along the sides of the Merced River on Highway

Oldest rocks of the Yosemite region — black slates seen along the Merced River and Highway 140, of Paleozoic age. (There are Precambrian rocks outside the park boundaries.)

(From color slide by the writer)

135

140, a few miles west of Arch Rock Entrance. Here they are glossy black slates, but may be of reddish color in cracks where the iron has oxidized. Within the river bed they have been leached to shades of gray.

During the Mesozoic Triassic and Jurassic Periods time was provided for these folded sediments to have become eroded away again to sea level, allowing a second marine invasion to occur, spreading sands, muds, and volcanic materials upon their submerged, tilted strata. At about the end of the Jurassic Period these layers were again uplifted and folded, accompanied by intrusions of granite known as the Sierra Nevada batholith, forming a second ancestral mountain range. Much of this structure fractured into cracks, into which fluid magma also pressed its way forming dikes varying in thickness from an inch or so to several feet, and often to hundreds of feet in length.

Once again stream erosion tore down these formations, exposing the granites within the mountain cores, during most of Cretaceous time, which ended about 65 million years ago. By then the region was a peneplane of rolling hills extending in a northwesterly direction.

The Cenozoic Era, beginning with the early Tertiary Period, brought uplift and southwestward tilting to the area, causing most of the rivers to divert their channels toward the west. Among these was the early Merced River, at first meandering through a wide valley, but cutting deeper as the upwarping continued, not at once, but in many stages. During Pliocene time the Sierra Block remained comparatively quiet, while the Merced River continued its production of a steeply walled canyon of more than a thousand feet in depth. About two million years ago, closing the Pliocene, a series of uplifts raised the Sierra Nevada Block to its present height of above 14,000 feet, while the Merced valley simultaneously cut its depth to 1500 feet, although tributary valleys were unable to keep pace with their parent stream, so were left hanging high up on the canyon walls. Such discrepant elevations at tributary mouths were increased still more by the glaciation which was yet to come.

Glaciation

The Pleistocene Ice Age brought three distinct times of glacial ice invasion into the Yosemite region. Each glacial stage lasted for many thousand years, separated from the next by interglacial stages of equal durations.

The first two stages were of longest duration and caused greatest erosion. Yosemite Valley was filled rim to rim with ice, covering Glacier Point to a 500 foot depth, although some of the higher peaks, such as El Capitan, Half Dome, and Sentinel Dome, were left as summits protruding above the surface of the ice. These glaciers extended to the southwest as far as El Portal, where the warmer temperatures at only 2000 feet elevation caused melting to occur. Tongues of ice also entered the main valley from the upper Merced and Tenaya Canyons.

The major V-shaped gorge cut by the Merced River became deepened perhaps 2000 feet, and eroded into a typical U-shape, always so indicative of glaciation. Tributary valleys, containing less ice, were deepened less, and so Yosemite Falls, Bridalveil Fall, and others were left hanging even higher upon the canyon walls, where the high waterfalls characterizing Yosemite now drop a thousand feet or more down to the valley floor. The third glacial invasion was of less importance, filling the valley only about a third as deeply as those formerly, and extending only past El Capitan.

Moraines then began to form, sometimes damming the water behind them, as with Ancient Lake Yosemite, 5½ miles long to the head of the valley and about 2000 feet deep there, yet only a few hundred feet in depth near its lower end where accumulation of the debris was more rapid. The lake soon became sediment-filled and disappeared, leaving the present level valley floor atop thousands of feet of gravel, sand, and silt.

A few minor glaciers and icefields are yet existent in protected areas high among the mountains. Lyell Glacier, about a mile wide and half a mile long, is near the 13,114 foot summit of the mountain bearing the same name. Maclure Glacier is a similar example.

Waterfalls

Upper Yosemite Fall is 1430 feet high, the second highest free-leaping waterfall in the world. (Angel Fall in S.E. Venezuela is reputedly the highest, with an astounding fall of 2648 feet, plus a 564 foot lower drop.) Adding the above 1430 feet of Upper Fall to 675 feet for the Middle Cascades and another 320 feet for the Lower Fall makes a total of 2425 feet for Yosemite — among the world's highest.

Upper and Lower Yosemite Falls. Total height includes 1430 feet of Upper Fall, 675 feet of Middle Cascades, plus 320 feet of Lower Fall — a combined fall of 2425 feet, one of the world's major waterfalls.

Ribbon Fall, across the valley, is the highest single fall in the Park, at 1612 feet, but it is not entirely free of the cliff face.

Bridalveil Fall, near Cathedral Rocks, is another which drops 620 feet vertically out of its hanging valley. Vernal and Nevada Falls in the upper Merced valley leap down a gigantic stairway where the river has carved a channel over jointed blocks partially removed by glacial ice.

The Waterwheel Falls of the Tuolumne River are especially noteworthy, but are accessible only to hikers. As the river rapidly descends in Tuolumne Canyon, rocky obstructions cause the water to be deflected upward into picturesque arcs.

Rock Masses

The granitic rocks of Yosemite National Park occur in about twelve variations, which are therefore differently affected by factors of weathering, glacial erosion, exfoliation, and jointing.

Lack of jointing has formed El Capitan, said to be the most massive block of granite in the entire Sierra Nevada, 3604 feet in height. The almost vertical face of this monolith was once considered impossible to climb, but its first ascent was made in November, 1959, with several having been accomplished in later years. LIFE magazine recently pub - lished a detailed account of this climb, describing how the men spent two nights in hammocks suspended from pitons driven into the cliff. A much easier trail to the top can be followed from the back slopes, along a fairly steep hiking trail.

Liberty Cap and Mount Broderick became rounded from glacial erosion, but similar lack of jointing prevented formation of cliff faces.

Many cliffs, such as the side of Half Dome facing the valley (and by the way, the other "half" never did exist), have been produced by splitting along vertical joints, contrary to early theories that the cliff was a result of glacial erosion. In the first place, glaciers never reached the summit of Half Dome, and secondly, it is composed of a dense quartz monzonite, similar to granite, but much less susceptible to

El Capitan — a massive block of granite 3604 feet high. Its face has been climbed on various occasions since 1959.

erosion. The cliffs at Glacier Point, Upper Yosemite Fall, and Ribbon Fall are also due to this type of jointing.

Sometimes several sets of joints exist in different directions, producing such forms as Cathedral Rocks, Washington Column, or Sentinel Rock.

Half Dome and others of its type were formed by exfoliation, not fully understood, by which curved sheets or shells of rocks were loosened from the surface of the larger mass. Former theories ascribed this action to changes in temperature, expansion due to hydration, or tension cracks during cooling of the igneous mass. Modern belief inclines toward a theory of "load relief," meaning that as outer layers are stripped away, deeper portions will swell under release of stress, with fractures parallel to the surface to continue the process.

Half Dome — a granite mass characterized by hemispherical exfoliated layers, but not eroded off by glaciation, as often believed. No "other half" ever existed.

NEVADA

LEHMAN CAVES National Monument (Ground Water)

Soon after crossing the Utah-Nevada boundary via U.S. 6-50, and travelling thence on Nevada 73 to Baker, then westward on Nevada 74 for about 5 miles, one may well enjoy a visit to Lehman Caves, Nevada's only National Park or Monument except for that portion of Death Valley included within the state. One writer has described it as the "gem" of all National Park Service caves, even though it is much smaller than the famed Carlsbad Caverns of New Mexico. It is located on the east slope of Wheeler Peak, the 13,063 foot pinnacle of the Snake Range.

Lehman Caves have been formed in a compressed, metamorphic white to light-gray limestone or marble, probably of mid-Cambrian age. It overlies a thick quartzite, and although a granitic intrusion near the contact did not affect the previously metamorphosed quartzite much, it did recrystallize some of the limestone into marble.

As with any cave, ground water charged with carbon dioxide penetrated the marble, dissolving material from the cracks throughout, and eventually creating chambers and passageways. Subsequent seepages of ground water entered these openings from above, allowing the carbon dioxide to escape, with simultaneous precipitation of calcium carbonate as calcite crystals, varied in shape and color, completely covering the ceilings and walls of the rooms and adjoining passages.

Stalactites by the thousand developed, hanging pendant from the ceilings; water dripping from them created the chunky, compact stalagmites rising from the floor, often joining in columnar formation.

Helictites grow in root-like formations from the walls; draperies like curtains line the passages; pools of water are self-dammed with terraced deposits. Colors range from a creamy white through orange or red to chocolate brown. Thin discs called shields or palletes are found in unusual angular arrangement over walls and floors. Notably, Lehman Caves are "live," as water continues to build these formations throughout the indefinite future.

Delicate columns of limestone formed by the conjunction of stalactites forming from the ceiling with stalagmites developing upward from the floor.   (National Park Service)

ARIZONA

CHIRICAHUA National Monument (Volcanism, Erosion)

In southern Arizona, about 96 miles southeast of Tucson, is Chiricahua National Monument. One word might be used to typify the scenery here: rocks! The whole monument of 17 square miles is a mass of pinnacles, weird rock shapes resembling men and beasts, balanced rocks, and other forms beyond one's wildest imagination.

Tertiary flows, mostly of rhyolitic molded tuff from a light colored silicic magma, spread out over level land. Very little basalt is present. The process of cooling produced many contractional crackings in a multitude of patterns, and subsequent uplifts of the region raised these into a mountainous topography. Finally, erosion by air and moisture resulted in an assemblage of monolithic figures amid canyons cut into the deep flows of Miocene age.

The scenic area is at the western edge of the Chiricahua Mountains, where Chiricahua Peak reaches an elevation of 9798 feet. The high elevation causes rain clouds to gather and drop their refreshing moisture to a more abundant extent hereabouts than in the semi-arid plains surrounding the region. For this reason many unusual types of animal and plant life are found here in this oasis-like location, unknown elsewhere nearby.

The monument road ascends a high ridge out of Bonita Canyon, continuing to the parking area near Sugarloaf Mountain, whose summit (Elev. 7308 feet) can be reached by a hiking trail. At the end of the road is Masai Point, where a magnificent view is seen. Another trail from here crosses the canyon and continues into the "Heart of Rocks" area, a mass of pinnacles partially covered with lichens. "Big Balanced Rock," pictured on the next page, can be seen here, together with other picturesquely named formations such as "Punch and Judy," "Duck on a Rock," etc.

Such formations occur when two resistant layers of rock are separated by a softer type. Weathering usually erodes rapidly into the softer stratum, and the uppermost boulders topple sooner or later. In a few cases, weathering takes place so evenly that a temporary pedestal beneath the upper

144

block leaves it in a balanced position. Such formations are fairly common in the Rocky Mountain states, the best known example being in the Garden of the Gods, in Colorado.

"Big Balanced Rock," formed by erosion of a resistant formation above a softer formation underneath. All such must fall eventually.

(From color slide from Ward's Nat. Sci. Est.)

GRAND CANYON National Monument (Sedimentation, Diastrophism, Volcanism, Erosion)

Grand Canyon National Monument, established in 1932, includes an additional area of 310 square miles to the west of Grand Canyon National Park, and contains 40 miles of the Colorado River gorge. It is accessible only from the north side, usually via Kanab, Utah and Fredonia, Arizona, thence by graded road for 65 miles southward to the Tuweap Ranger Station, and finally over 6 miles of unimproved road not advisable for travel in bad weather, and not without difficulty at any time. Thus the area is not yet recommended to the general public.

The general geology of the canyon here is of course identical with that farther upstream in the Park, except that there is more evidence of volcanic activity in the Monument subsequent to the formation of the main canyon and its tributary canyons. A volcanic field on both sides of the river, extending beyond the western end of the monument, formed the Pine Mountains which contained many craters. Very hot lava flows poured over both canyon walls, also down a canyon on the north side which is now known as Toroweap Valley. Mount Trumbull, about 12 miles north of Toroweap Point and outside the monument's boundaries, was one of the major volcanic craters.

The lava flows often blocked the river below, creating dams which were later eroded through, forming rapids in the channel.

The canyon is more narrow here than anywhere in the Park itself, and a superb vista of the Inner Gorge presents itself to the adventurous visitor. The main attraction is Toroweap Point, where a sheer rock cliff almost 3000 feet high overlooks the windings of the Colorado River far below. This is pictured on the next page.

Grand Canyon National Monument, according to Senate Bill No. 1296, was added to Grand Canyon National Park on January 3, 1975. The monument now has no individual identity.

View at Toroweap Point downward toward the Colorado River, about 3000 feet below,

(National Park Service)

GRAND CANYON National Park
(Sedimentation, Diastrophism, Erosion)

"Golly, what a gully!" a teen-ager is said to have exclaimed at her first sight of northern Arizona's Grand Canyon of the Colorado River. The first comments of the Spanish Conquistadors upon reaching the South Rim in 1540 were not recorded, but perhaps were similar. Three members, it is said, made an unsuccessful attempt to reach the river seen far below.

Spanish missionary priests came here in 1776, and American trappers and hunters of the next half century told stories of the huge gorge. Many considered it primarily as a very annoying obstruction to travel in a north-south direction because of the impossibility of crossing it anywhere within many miles.

A War Department expedition in 1857-58 ascended the Colorado River, examining fossils, rocks, and stratigraphic features, and reported their definite conclusion that the river itself had eroded the main canyon and its tributaries.

In 1869 and again in 1871 Major John Wesley Powell's party made their famous and daring descents of the canyon by boat, furnishing much further information. They were quite convinced that the river's present winding route toward the Gulf of California had developed many millions of years ago on a low flood plain, to be uplifted later in two stages while the river continued its downward entrenchment at an equal rate. This geological explanation of the Colorado River as an antecedent stream, thus forming the chasm walls, the middle plateau, and the inner gorge was considered authentic for decades.

Present theories relate the river to superposed origin, rather than antecedent. A layman's distinction between these might be summarized by stating that a truly antecedent stream, such as the Columbia River transversing the Cascade Range, had developed its channel first, with the mountains then being raised slowly across its path, while a superposed stream, like those crossing the Appalachian Mountains, has lowered its channel by erosion onto previously folded strata.

Latest research has proven that the uplift of the Kaibab Plateau occurred much less recently than had been supposed, probably about 65 million years ago when the Laramide Revolution raised the modern Rocky Mountains at the close of the Mesozoic Era. At this time, it is believed, the Colorado did not flow into the Gulf of California, but deposited its sediments into a number of interior drainage lakes such as Lake Bidahochi on the Navajo Indian Reservation. Another westward stream, the Hualapai, cut headward across the Kaibab Plateau until by geological piracy it beheaded the Upper Colorado and diverted its waters into the Gulf of California, while the lower portion reversed its course to become the present Little Colorado, now a tributary of the major stream.

The most noteworthy single feature of the Grand Canyon is undoubtedly its tremendous vertical exposure of sedimentary strata. The history of the earth can be interpreted much more completely from such materials than from igneous or metamorphic types. About 95% of the upper 10 miles of the earth's crust is igneous in origin, but of the rocks exposed at the surface, 75% are sedimentary.

Sedimentary rocks have been accumulating ever since rainfall began on our planet, and it has been estimated that perhaps 500,000 feet, or 100 miles, of strata have been deposited. Of course, no single area displays this complete section, or even an appreciable part of it. Much has been eroded away, as indicated by stratigraphic gaps between the layers present, which sometimes represent an interval of many hundreds of millions of years. Existing strata must be studied under one of two conditions: either when tilted at an angle along a horizontal surface, or when cut vertically through the layers. In the Grand Canyon about 4000 feet are thus exposed to view, depicting a sequence of nearly 2 billion years, lying unconformably above another 1000 feet of Precambrian igneous and metamorphic rocks, greatly folded into angular positions.

A simplified diagram of the cross section of the canyon wall at the Kaibab Trail is shown here, based on a National Park Service Pamphlet.

Detailed discussion of the history and nature of these formations being available in so many sources, only the briefest possible commentary on each will be stated here chronologically.

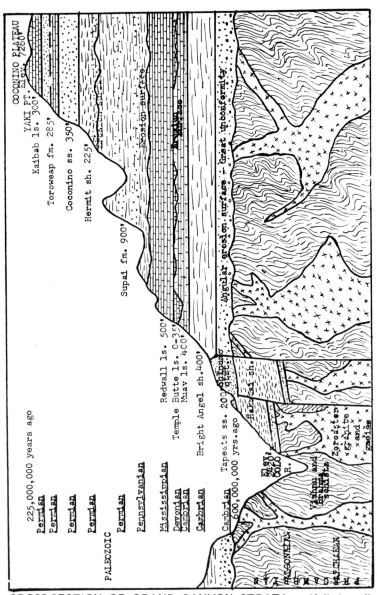

CROSS-SECTION OF GRAND CANYON STRATA — Kaibab trail, South Rim. (Slightly modified by writer after N.P.S. Bull. 1966, p.11)

View down Bright Angel trail from near El Tovar Hotel on the South Rim. Indian Gardens may be seen about halfway down, the lunch stop for mule trains and riders. It is located on the ancient Cambrian flood plain.

PRECAMBRIAN (ARCHEAN AND ALGONKIAN) ERAS

The dark colored dense rocks in the gorge, now standing in twisted, approximately vertical layers (Vishnu schist) were at one time horizontal deposits eroded from some unknown pre-existing mountain-like mass. Lavas (Brahma schist) were mingled among these. Intrusions of lighter, coarse-grained reddish pegmatite granite (Zoroaster granite) were thrust into them. Mountain building (Mazatzal Revolution) raised and contorted the structure into a range as high as any existing today, recrystallizing and folding the sediments seen at the bottom of the canyon. Some black and white hornblende gneisses are included.

After the surface of the mountain mass had been eroded to a practically level surface, a shallow sea invaded the area, forming the Bass limestone. Here are found rippled and mud-cracked layers, also indications of limestone reefs formed by algae, the first evidence of life. A bright red mud, the Hakatai shale, also showing similar evidences of shallow water origin, was a thick deposit over the limestone, indicating the withdrawal of the sea. Finally, a coarse sandstone, now compressed into the Shinumo quartzite, was laid down as the water became still more shallow toward the shore line. All of these Upper Precambrian (Algonkian) formations are grouped into the Grand Canyon Series.

Another interval of mountain building took place, known as the Grand Canyon Revolution, yet again erosion reduced the region to a level surface, with ridges of more resistant rock remaining here and there. The first layers of Paleozoic deposits (Cambrian) lie horizontally upon these tilted strata at abrupt angles with those below. This is known as the Great Unconformity, easily seen along the canyon walls, and represents a missing interval of probably 500 million years, during which erosion removed many thousand feet of the older rocks. Disconformities, also existent in the Grand Canyon walls, are those sequences of strata when both are relatively horizontal, yet are separated by an irregular erosional surface.

Precambrian granite and gneiss at river level in the Colorado River
gorge. The river is at low stage.

PALEOZOIC ERA

The entire valley wall above the inner gorge is composed of Paleozoic sedimentary beds, deposited during that era between about 600 million and 225 million years ago. They all lie horizontally, although some strata are separated by an erosion irregularity of surface, indicative of uplift, erosion, or both. Such gaps in the stratigraphic record, known as disconformities, show that either the corresponding sediments were never deposited, or if so, were completely eroded away afterward.

Cambrian Period
Directly upon the Great Unconformity surface was laid the Tapeats sandstone, a very coarse-grained beach deposit about 200 feet thick containing fossil shells, seaweed imprints, and ripple marks. About this lie 400 feet of the Bright Angel shale, a greenish-gray silt deposit containing marine fossils. Overlying this is about 400 feet of buff lime in the Muav formation, formed as the sea grew deeper. These layers form the surface of the benchland called the Tonto Platform, a former flood plain of the river. Indian Gardens make a shady rest area here.

Ordovician and Silurian Periods
These intervals of time, totalling about 175 million years, were primarily erosional, and if any deposits were formed, no record remains.

Central and Eastern states, however, do contain many thousands of feet of strata deposited in these periods, ranging from oil-bearing shales and limestones to shallow-water salt beds.

Devonian Period
The Temple Butte limestone formed at this time is not abundant in the canyon. It is lavender or purplish color, notably containing some fossil remains of primitive armored fishes, also corals and other invertebrates. It is not visible along the Bright Angel Trail, but there is a minor occurrence on the Kaibab Trail.

154

Mississippian Period

The Redwall limestone, averaging more than 500 feet thick, is a remarkable cliff-building formation in the canyon, corresponding in general to the 2000-foot Madison limestone of the Montana and Wyoming Rockies. It is quite fossiliferous, containing invertebrate corals, brachiopods, and crinoids. The normal color is a bluish-gray where freshly broken, but most surfaces are reddish because of iron oxide staining from the red shales above.

Here is a good place to explain why the walls of the Grand Canyon are alternately perpendicular, then at a slant. The vertical surfaces are of cliff-building formations, resistant to erosion, while the slopes are made of the softer shales, separated by the harder limestones and sandstones.

Pennsylvanian Period

Following another erosion gap, there was again a subsiding of the land, and the lower portion of the Supai formation was laid in a shallow sea, mainly as a limy shale.

Permian Period

The Supai formation continues quietly into the next, or Permian Period, with modification of the deposits into about 1000 feet of reddish sandy shales, a typical shore line deposit. It often contains tracks of four-footed animals, sometimes with traces of having a dragging tail, — probably amphibians. It also contains remains of fern-like plants.

The Hermit shale continues above another erosional surface, also of a dark red color, with a thickness of perhaps 300 feet. Many have difficulty in distinguishing these two formations, even at close view along the trail, but in general the Hermit shale is of a finer muddy texture and a deeper red color. It is a similar freshwater deposit containing the same types of fossils.

The Coconino sandstone predominates in all pictures of Grand Canyon walls. It is a thick white or buff layer extending horizontally about 600 feet below the top of the plateau, and is a deposit of wind-blown desert sand showing much typical cross-bedding. Perhaps 300 feet thick in the eastern portion of the canyon, it tapers to less than 100 feet in the western section. Footprints of primitive reptiles, also trails of scorpions, insects, and worms are present.

The Toroweap formation is more difficult to identify, consisting of about 250 feet of yellow and red sandstones above and below, with a gray limestone layer in between. It was formed in a warm shallow sea which developed upon the sand dunes, creating a level surface upon which the sands and lime mark the advance and withdrawal of the sea. Brachiopod and mollusk fossils are abundant within it.

The Kaibab limestone is the surface formation of both the Coconino Plateau south of Grand Canyon and the Kaibab Plateau to the northward. It marks the enroachment of the Kaibab Sea across the region, the last of such during the Paleozoic era, which ended about 225 million years ago. It is a buff to creamy white color, also fossiliferous.

View down the South Kaibab trail and across Grand Canyon. Trail begins at Yaki Point, and is steeper than Bright Angel trail. WARNING: There is no drinking water along this trail!   (National Park Service)

MESOZOIC ERA

Mesozoic strata at one time covered all this area to a depth of at least 4000 feet, but have almost all been eroded entirely away. One butte, Cedar Mountain, which is near the eastern edge of the Park and easily visible from Desert View and the Watchtower, is composed of the Moenkopi formation red shales, capped by a layer of the pebbly Shinarump conglomerate. Both of these are non-marine formations of Triassic age. A similar Mesozoic outcrop is Red Butte, along the south approach to the Park, about 15 miles from Grand Canyon Village. Here the Moenkopi formation is capped by a layer of Tertiary lava which reduces erosion of this remnant.

Cedar Mountain, northeast of Desert View Watchtower. This is one of the few remnants of Mesozoic strata over the area.

(From telephoto view color slide by the writer)

CENOZOIC ERA

The Grand Canyon region has been much uplifted above sea level during the entire Cenozoic era of the last 65 million years, so the process of erosion has been dominant. Some volcanic lava flows poured down the canyon walls, damming the river and forming the rapids seen today toward the west, as discussed for Grand Canyon National Monument. Some fresh water lake beds were formed by the ancestral Colorado River southeast of the Park, such as the Bidahochi formation previously mentioned. Related delta deposits downstream, the Muddy Creek formation, have been radiometrically dated as about 10 million years old, indicating the time required to cut the Grand Canyon.

The Grand Canyon averages 9 miles in width and a mile in depth, with a river length of 217 miles. The South Rim has a U.S. Bench Mark of 6866 feet at El Tovar Hotel, while that at Grand Canyon Lodge on the North Rim likewise is one marked 8153 feet above sea level. An experienced hiker could traverse the distance between these by following the Bright Angel trail 8 miles to the river, then 3 miles along the River Trail, crossing the famous suspension bridge pictured below, then the more difficult 14 mile North Kaibab Trail

Approaching the Colorado River suspension bridge along the descent of the South Kaibab trail.

158

which crosses Bright Angel Creek four times. Yet by car the distance between these hotels is 214 miles!

This 1300-foot difference in elevation is merely due to the southward dipping slope of the Phantom monocline, with 9000-foot elevations still farther north. It is definitely not due to a geologic fault extending lengthwise of the canyon, as some think. True, many faults do cross the canyon, including the major Bright Angel fault and the parallel minor ones a few miles apart, such as Crystal, Hermit, and Vishnu faults.

Past records indicate a wide variation in the amount of water and sediment coursing through the canyon, from only 700 cubic feet of water per second on December 28, 1924, to 127,000 cubic feet per second on July 2, 1927. The sediment load figures just prior to completion of the Glen Canyon dam upstream showed an average daily load of 425,000 tons.

Since construction of this dam, Lake Powell absorbs about three-fourths of the sediment from the river, resulting in a greenish color for the lower stream instead of its former muddy brown hue. This will also prolong the life of Lake Mead, above Hoover Dam, to an estimated several hundred years, in contrast to its former rate of rapid filling.

MARBLE CANYON National Monument (Erosion)

Marble Canyon is another quite recent addition to NPS areas, proclaimed in January, 1969. It contains slightly more than 26,000 acres along a 50-mile stretch of the Colorado River in northern Arizona between Glen Canyon National Recreation Area and Grand Canyon National Park.

Leaving U.S. 89 at Bitter Springs, a U-shaped contour bend in U.S. 89A takes one upstream about 10 miles, then drops from the reddish surface of the Triassic Moenkopi beds down to the Navajo Bridge crossing the canyon, 467 feet above the river, and 616 feet long.

Navajo Bridge over Colorado River at Marble Canyon, north of Cameron, Arizona, on Highway 89.   (National Park Service)

This is the only bridge crossing the Colorado River within about 1000 miles. Here the cliffs are formed by the two Upper Permian formations, the Kaibab limestone and the Coconino sandstone. Farther downstream, approximately across from Point Imperial on the North Rim of Grand

Canyon and near the Park boundary, Marble Canyon — also sometimes called Upper Grand Canyon — reaches a spectacular 3000-foot depth. This is nearly as much as at Toroweap Point.

Marble Canyon National Monument, according to Senate Bill No. 1296, was added to Grand Canyon National Park on January 3, 1975. The monument now has no individual identity.

(METEOR CRATER — Mineralogy, Astronomy)

Arizona's world-famous meteor crater is not among the NPS Monuments, where it might well be except for being privately owned by the Barringer Crater Company, formerly the Standard Iron Company, founded by Daniel Moreau Barringer in 1903. Barringer was a Philadelphia mining engineer who died in 1929, a short time after the great market crash. He had devoted much of his life and private capital to attain recognition of his conviction that this pockmark on the earth's surface was indeed the result of a meteoric impact, rather than volcanic.

A description of this unique geologic feature is here included as an exception to the general content of this booklet, because of its interest to students of geology as well as vacationing visitors.

Commonly called Meteor Crater, this is actually a misnomer, since technically the word "meteor" applies only to the object during its incandescent path through the atmosphere, with "meteorite" being applicable only to those having struck the earth as solids. Arizona's example is not only the first proven meteorite, but also probably the world's largest, although others are known in various states and countries.

View of Meteor Crater from north rim, showing site of Barringer's first shaft attempted, 200 feet deep. See lower right of photo.

As seen from I-40 west of Winslow, and 6 miles north of the site, the low 150-foot, level-rim hillock presents an unimpressive aspect. From the rim, however, the view is more astonishing, the crater being 4150 feet in diameter and 570 feet deep, with steeply-walled sides.

The immense pit was first discovered by white men in 1871, and for years thereafter was considered as volcanic in origin, like so many other craters in the state. In 1902 Barringer's studies convinced him that a huge iron-type meteorite lay beneath the surface, and after purchasing the supposedly worthless land, he organized the Standard Iron Company to begin exploration work.

The surface geology is primarily that of the brick-red Triassic Moenkopi formation, uniformly covering the flat mesa. In a gully eroded east of the crater, and swinging around twenty-odd miles more to the westward, the buff Permian Kaibab limestone is at the surface, as at the Grand Canyon. Underlying this is the Coconino sandstone, and finally, marking the lowest stratum into which the meteorite penetrated, is the red Supai shaly formation. All around the rim are large boulders of the Kaibab limestone which were hurled upward and outward at the time of impact, as proven by meteoritic fragments of iron-nickel material which have been found lying beneath them.

Barringer's first efforts consisted of digging trenches in the rim's outer slopes, uncovering more boulders and meteoritic fragments. The nearly round shape of the crater caused his first belief that the meteor had fallen vertically, so he began sinking a shaft in the center of the pit, as illustrated. Remains of the machinery may still be seen there.

At about 200-foot depth, water and quicksand halted this operation. Various strata, including pulverized Coconino sandstone as well as iron-nickel particles, were found throughout the hole. Exploratory holes were drilled within the crater to depths of more than 1000 feet, reaching the undisturbed Supai formation, and thus proving that the striking force had come from above.

Later studies indicated that a slanting impact could also have produced a round hole, as with a bullet shot into mud, and a 6-inch churn drill began operations midway of the south rim. Progress became increasingly difficult as resistant fragments of meteoritic material were encountered, and at a depth of 1376 feet the drill became stuck, the cable broke, and the hole was abandoned in August, 1922. Other drilling operations south of the rim were attempted, but lack of funds and the sudden death of Barringer forced the project to cease temporarily.

Subsequent geophysical and gravimetric surveys have been conducted, seemingly indicative of a huge high-gravity mass lying below, weighing perhaps 2 million tons. Various fragments found in the vicinity, presumably of the same origin, show an analysis of 91-92% iron, 7% nickel, and 1-2% of other elements, including minor but possibly valuable amounts of platinum, iridium, and traces of gold and silver. At the museum may be seen many such specimens, of which the largest weighs 1406 pounds.

Largest meteorite found within the area, weighing 1406 pounds, with others to be seen in the visitors' museum. (From color slide by the writer)

There are many scientists, however, who are convinced that the greater part of the mass was vaporized by heat developed at time of impact. Still others favor the belief that the original body consisted of a cluster of fragments hurtling through space.

This particular fall in Arizona seems almost certainly to have come from a northerly direction, imbedding itself beneath the south rim. The time of such occurrence is difficult to calculate, estimates having varied from 700 years to 75,000 years ago. Latest studies, including a Carbon-14 test, suggest a reasonable possibility as about 20,000 years ago. Some Indian legends are said to refer to a fall of fire from the sky, making a loud noise.

Meteorites are classified into three divisions: (a) stony, comprising more than 90% of the total, (b) a minor number of a stony-iron mixture, and (c) a larger proportion of iron-nickel type, usually containing 7-15% nickel alloyed with iron. The Barringer site, it is claimed, has furnished more of this metallic type than the rest of the world together.

The origin of meteors is not certainly known, but studies of various falls suggest that they may originate in the zone of small planetoids between Mars and Jupiter, where many astronomers believe a typical planet once existed. Like our Earth, it may have had a rocky surface and an iron-nickel core, subsequently having been disrupted because of some unknown cause.

Other officially recognized single or grouped craters are known in the countries of Arabia, Argentina, Australia, Estonia, Siberia, Tasmania, and the United States. The last include, besides that in Arizona, others in Texas and Kansas. Among single meteorites, the largest American ones were taken to the Hayden Planetarium of New York City from Greenland (weight: 33.1 tons), and from the Willamette Valley of Oregon (weight: 14.2 tons).

PETRIFIED FOREST National Park
(Mineralogy, Paleontology)

Much of the literature on Petrified Forest refers to it as a National Monument, and it is true that it was created as one of the earliest of these among a group in 1906, following the passage of the National Antiquities Act. However, in 1958 Congress passed an act stating that when all private holdings within the Monument had been acquired by the Federal Government, and notice of such completion had appeared in the federal register, the Monument would become a National Park. This notice appeared on November 8, 1962, and the Monument became a Park on December 9, 1962.

Some writers have described this area as containing the most spectacular display of petrified wood anywhere in the world. Petrified wood may be found in almost every state and country known, but here the translucency and brilliancy of the colors far surpass the opaque browns and grays more usually noted.

A portion of the Painted Desert is located within Petrified Forest, about 27 miles east of Holbrook, Arizona,

Southern portion of the Painted Desert, located within the Petrified Forest area. It is composed of vari-colored shales of Triassic (Chinle) age, containing gypsum crystals. (From color slide from Ward's Nat. Sci. Est.)

166

and north of I-40. This is the part of Painted Desert most commonly viewed from the rim drive, but it also extends almost 10 miles northward.

Geologic History
The Painted Desert is nearly all formed of the Triassic Chinle formation, plus surficial alluvial soils, consisting of maroon and gray shales with sparkling diamond-shaped crystals of gypsum (hydrous calcium sulfate), most vividly seen in early morning or late afternoon, especially after a shower.

South of I-40, the Triassic Moenkopi formation covers much of the surface, with the log-bearing Chinle beds exposed lower in the stream-cut gullies. The petrified portions of trees consist almost entirely of logs, with practically no root segments or branches to be seen. This, plus other evidence, indicates that the trees did not grow originally in the Park area, but more probably about 100 miles to the west and southwest. They belong mostly to an extinct species of a pine *(Araucarioxylon)*, of which related species still grow in South America, Australia, and the South Pacific islands.

These were of Triassic age, dated at about 160-170 million years ago, growing on a low, swampy flood plain. Streams from low hills nearby deposited tremendous amounts of mud and sand, which especially contained much volcanic ash, largely silica. As the trees died from various causes, such as high winds, floods, or volcanism in addition to natural biologic reasons, their trunks were picked up by flood waters, rolled along while being denuded of branches and bark, finally to be left in the delta area. Much ash became decomposed into a clay-like soil called Bentonite, which absorbed many colored tints of iron oxides and other minerals, characterizing the Painted Desert. About 300-400 feet of such deposits collected as the Chinle formation, widely spread over western New Mexico and eastern Arizona.

Gradual subsidence of the area allowed the shallow Cretaceous seas to come in during the following millions of years, finally burying the Triassic formations under 3000 feet of marine sediments. At the close of the era, marked by the rise of the Rocky Mountains, uplift of the region brought

167

about erosion of these sediments, again exposing the Chinle strata with its logs now petrified through infiltration of siliceous matter into the cell spaces of the woody tissue. The material now comprises about 98% mineral deposit, mainly quartz and its varieties such as chalcedony and jasper.

There are six distinct forests to be seen, formerly numerically designated, but now known as:

Jasper Forest, with Agate Bridge nearby, which is a log 4 feet thick and 111 feet long, spanning a 44 foot gully.

Blue Forest, 3 miles from Agate Bridge.

Black Forest, across I-40 in the Painted Desert, and relatively inaccessible except to experienced hikers.

Crystal Forest, 6 miles from the Park headquarters and museum.

Long Logs Forest, near the museum, obviously named for the length of its logs.

Giant Logs Forest, adjacent to the museum, where toward the rear is the large Old Faithful Log, showing butt and attached roots.

Petrified Forest Terrain — log sections are contained within the Triassic (Chinle) formation. WARNING: VISITORS ARE FORBIDDEN TO REMOVE SPECIMENS! (They may be purchased from areas outside National Park boundaries.) National Park Service

While the National Antiquities Act passed by Congress on June 8, 1906 was most specifically aimed at vandalism of archeological ruins of the Southwest, it definitely provides severe penalties for removing any samples or specimens from any National Park or Monument.

Many signs warn visitors that removal of the wood is a federal offense and request that observed thefts be reported to the rangers. Yet in spite of closing the park between sunset and sunrise, and completely fencing it off, thefts of wood continue. In the first nine months of 1972, 1950 pounds of wood were confiscated from 260 visitors, and $1850 in fines were paid. At either end of the Park signs warn: "Inspection station ahead," and in 1971 3850 pounds of fragments were found thrown nearby by people who apparently had changed their minds. One ranger suggests that the time may come when all visitors' cars will be parked outside, with guided bus tours being operated.

Petrified sections of logs, now mineralized to jasper, agate, or chalcedony, lying here and there upon the hilly surface.

(National Park Service)

SUNSET CRATER National Monument
(Volcanism, Archeology)

About 600 A.D. a small group of agricultural Indians of the pit house culture (see Mesa Verde National Park) occupied an area near the San Francisco Peaks north of Flagstaff. This region had been intermittently volcanically active for the last million years or so. Because of the poor soil and the dry climate they made only limited progress.

Then about 900 years ago, probably in the fall of 1064 A.D. as determined by tree-ring dating, they must have stared aghast at a volcanic eruption which suddenly developed near the eastern portion of the peaks. Ashes and cinders poured down upon their homes, and after the explosive violence had lessened, lava flows from basal vents continued. Finally, as the magma subsided, vapors and hot springs near the crest produced the yellow sulfur-stained rocks and pink to red ash deposits which have suggested the name for the peak.

Sunset Crater, a recently eruptive volcanic peak, as seen from the south.

(From color slide from Ward's Nat. Sci. Est.)

The crater is now about 400 feet deep, highest on the northeast rim because of the southwesterly winds. The black lava flows and cinder fields toward the base appear as though cooled only recently. A small lava cave near the foot of the peak contains a perpetual mass of ice, similar to those of Craters of the Moon in Idaho, or the Zuni Mountains of New Mexico.

Like a blessing in disguise, the weathered cinders and ash improved the land, and the Indians returned in even greater numbers, building many villages, such as Wupatki, in the vicinity. The porosity of the material aided in conservation of the moisture, and its mulching action improved the soil. During the 12th century, Wupatki contained more than 100 rooms, housing up to 300 people. But by 1200 A.D., the winds had stripped away much of the cinder covering, and the great drought of 1276-1299 caused the departure of the entire group. The ruins of Wupatki are now preserved as an archeological National Monument.

NEW MEXICO

CAPULIN MOUNTAIN National Monument (Volcanism)

As one follows U.S. 64-87 across northeastern New Mexico between Raton and Clayton, a beautifully symmetrical cinder cone is seen near the highway. It was an early landmark for pioneers heading westward. From its base there extends a mass of jumbled basalt formed by a typical lava flow.

The mountain rises at least 1000 feet above the plain, with a rim 1450 feet in diameter, and a crater 415 feet deep. From its top, at 8215 feet elevation, five states can be seen if the atmosphere is clear: New Mexico, Texas, Oklahoma, Kansas and Colorado.

Capulin Mountain, active about 7000 years ago, viewed from the south along U.S. 87, near Raton, N.M.   (National Park Service)

Capulin typifies the final stages of widespread volcanic activity in western North and South America after the glaciers had left most of the continents. Several other peaks to the northwest were formed during this same activity, in which lava flows occurred intermittently, separated by times of erosion. Capulin was formed during the last of these eruptive periods, of which there were at least three. The highest mesas, uplifted and eroded, now expose the oldest lavas, while the later eruptions included more ash and cinders.

Studies indicate that Capulin became active only about 7000 years ago. Its sides are still so steep that boulders occasionally roll down, and some of the exposures are so glassy that they appear to have cooled only recently. However, much more recent flows only 1000 to 2000 years old are known in New Mexico, as near Grants and Carrizoso.

A spiral road allows the ascent of a vehicle to the very top of Capulin Mountain, so that with the highway so near, this is one of the most typical and accessible volcanic cones for study.

CARLSBAD CAVERNS National Park (Ground Water)

Carlsbad Caverns in southeastern New Mexico, situated 18 miles from the city of Carlsbad on U.S. 62-180, is open daily throughout the year and is among the most popular of our national resorts. There is a stable cave temperature of 56°F., although weather outside has ranged from −10°F. to 108°F. in the last 40 years.

According to recent park statistics, the tally of visitors from all over the world approaches three quarters of a million. Daily visitations total around 2000, with an average of 250–300 persons per walking tour. The largest travel day recorded was July 3, 1966 — the 50th anniversary year — when 9,308 visitors entered the caverns. Because of the increased number of daily visitors, all leave now via the passenger elevators.

Visitors grouped along the entrance trail into Carlsbad Caverns. Note Park Ranger at upper left.   (From color slide by the writer)

174

Cavern Chemistry

The chemistry of cave deposits may be simplified by combining these word equations:

atmospheric carbon dioxide + water $\rightarrow$ carbonic acid

carbonic acid + limestone $\rightarrow$ soluble calcium bicarbonate

Precipitation of calcium carbonate or limestone results from loss of carbon dioxide by loss of hydrostatic pressure and lessened CO_2 pressure, as well as evaporation when the solution enters a cavern through ceiling or walls.

soluble calcium $\rightarrow$ carbon dioxide + water + calcium
bicarbonate   (gas)   carbonate*

*Result: a stalactite, stalagmite, etc. (precipitate)

Cavern Characteristics

Carlsbad Caverns are often compared to Mammoth Cave, Kentucky. Since neither one has been completely explored, it is impossible to say which is actually "the largest," or "the best." Each has certain features which surpass corresponding ones of the other, and each has unique configurations of its own.

Carlsbad undoubtedly possesses the world's largest underground chamber yet found, with its Big Room covering 14 acres, and having dimensions of nearly 4000 feet length, 625 feet width, and maximum ceiling height of 285 feet. It is approximately 750 feet below the surface.

The solution level called the Bat Cave is nearer the surface, approximately 160-180 feet underground. The lower level embracing the Scenic Rooms, including King's Palace and many others, is at about 830-850 feet beneath the surface. According to former Park superintendent Neal P. Guse, the deepest point in Carlsbad Caverns is "The Lake of the Clouds," where the water surface was found in 1966 to be at an elevation of 3,311.057 feet above sea level. This would correspond to an approximate "depth below surface" of between 1000 and 1100 feet.

King's Palace is the lowest cavern accessible to daily visitors, although at rare times specially guided tours into Lower Cave are offered to certain groups.

Details of the guided tour need not be described here, being readily available in free pamphlets and other references. Suffice it to state here that the map of Carlsbad Caverns is shaped like a huge L, with the leg starting from the Natural Entrance extending westward to the King's Palace area, and the other long wing then passing southward from the junction past the lunch room and elevators, through the Big Room to the Bottomless Pit at the southern extremity mid-point of the 1¼-mile round trip encircling the Big Room on its return.

Carlsbad Caverns also excels with its gigantic stalagmites, such as Temple of the Sun, Giant Dome, and Rock of Ages.

Entrance trail to the Big Room, with an area of about 14 acres, 750 feet below the surface. (From color slide by the writer)

"Rock of Ages," a large stalagmite. Some years ago it was the custom to ask visitors to seat themselves safely upon floor ledges, then all lights were turned out for one minute to demonstrate "total darkness," after which they were successively turned on from far down the trail, while a quartet of rangers sang "Rock of Ages." This beautiful custom has been discontinued because of increasing numbers of visitors — about 5000 per day. (National Park Service)

177

Geologic History

First, omitting more ancient and less relevant geologic events, the 1600 foot reef of Capitan limestone of Permian age was laid down under marine conditions about 200 million years ago at the edge of an inland arm of the sea. Second, sediments were deposited in the adjacent shallow lagoon, after which the sea level rose to cover the whole reef. Third, the Guadalupe uplift of the Rocky Mountain diastrophism, probably in the Miocene or Pliocene Epochs of the Tertiary Period, allowed water with its dissolved lime to pass outward, leaving the caverns behind. Fourth, ground water seeped through fractures in the surface limestones to reach the caverns' interiors, lose its carbon dioxide content, and then to deposit its mineral precipitates pendent from the ceilings as stalactites, or as dripped on downward to the floor to form the thicker, larger stalagmites within, as stated, probably the last 100,000 years.

Other types of lime configurations also occur, such as helictites against the walls, pillars, draperies, falls, or needle-like groupings. About 35 known caverns exist within the boundaries of the National Park. New Cave (formerly called Slaughter Cave from the canyon in which it is located) contains one pillar formed from the junction of a stalactite and a stalagmite which is 100 feet high and 18 feet in diameter.

The delicate tints of color characteristic of Carlsbad must be mentioned. Yellows, creams, pinks, grays, and pure whites can be seen throughout the various rooms, in contrast to the dull brownish-gray found more commonly in most caverns.

Crystal Spring Dome is the largest active formation in the caverns, 95% now being dry and static. It is the only formation in the cave for which a rate of growth has ever been carefully studied. Estimates place the growth of this dome at about 2½ cubic inches annually. Nevertheless, the tremendous tonnages of some of these formations must have been deposited within the last 100,000 years, as they rest upon fossils of that age.

Crystal Spring Dome — the largest actively growing stalagmite in the caverns — perhaps 2½ cu. in. annually.   (From color slide by the writer)

Bat Flights

Finally, the evening bat flights are among Carlsbad's most interesting sights. In all, about fourteen species of bats inhabit the cave at the upper level mentioned before. Of these, the Mexican free-tail bat is most common. At about sunset, visitors gather on the rock ledges surrounding the cave entrance to hear the ranger's lecture and to await, cameras ready, for the bats to appear. Then — one appears — then pairs, dozens — then hundreds of thousands spiralling counter-clockwise out of the entrance, almost like a black cloud in the sky. They spend the night seeking insects at the distant Black and Pecos Rivers, then return scatteringly at dawn.

Bat Flight at evening. They circle spirally upward from the entrance at sunset, search for insect food along the Black and Pecos Rivers during the night, then return at dawn, to sleep in a cavern apart from the visitor's trail. (National Park Service)

WHITE SANDS National Monument   (Erosion, Deposition)

No exaggeration is included in thus naming this unique scenic attraction of the southwest, for here is the world's largest surface deposit of glistening white crystals of gypsum, or hydrous calcium sulfate. Similar deposits are known in Utah and Australia. The monument's area of 228 square miles includes the most spectacular portion of the 275 square miles total deposits formed on and adjacent to the floor of ancient Lake Lucero. The last remnants of this exist as an intermittent lake in the southwest portion of the monument along U.S. 70-82 between Alamagordo and Las Cruces.

The general valley is known as the Tularosa Basin, bounded on the west by the San Andres Mountains and on the east by the Sacramento Mountains. Geologically, the area has sunk downward between the two fault scarps of the mountain fronts. These ranges consist mainly of Pennsylvanian and Permian strata, also Precambrian granites, lying beneath and along the foothills.

The gypsum originates in two major formations developed in the arid Permian Period as the Guadalupe Sea disappeared. They are the Whitehorse or Chalk Bluff gypsum of Guadalupian age and the lower gypsiferous shales, such as the Manzano gypsum of basal Yeso formation of Leonardian age. During the erosion of the mountains the gypsum has been dissolved and transported to the waters of Lake Lucero. Similar gypsum beds lie below the lake floor as well, further proof of the downward faulting of the whole basin. These mineral deposits reach the surface by capillary action upward through the soil.

As the lake water evaporates during the dry, windy season the lake becomes a crystal-encrusted marsh, and the gypsum crystals are loosened and blown over the basin by prevailing southwesterly winds. They accumulate in dune formation, like sand grains, and may have become stationary, or may still possess movement toward the northeast.

The dunes are not always continuous, but may be seen as undulating waves with bare ground between. Ripples mark their surfaces, and at times a visible cloud of particles may be noted moving up the windward sides and falling to the leeward. Average dune height is about 30 feet.

181

Interesting biological developments may be mentioned also. Stems of desert plants elongate with unusual rapidity to keep their crowns above ground, and root systems 40 feet in length have been noted. As the dune moves onward, pedestals of gypsum are left, bound together by the plant roots.

Animals likewise show modifications of their normal coloring as a result of nature's evolutionary development toward self-protection. The darker colored animals are easily discovered against the white background by hawks, foxes, or coyotes, and the lighter ones survive. As a result of such protective breeding through the centuries, pocket mice and lizards with a pale or almost white coloration are to be found here, whereas reddish colors prevail among the sand hills, and darker shades are known among the lava beds to the northward.

As a caution to visitors — do not try to drive cars with ordinary tires off the packed road surface. You may become stuck, spinning your wheels deeper and deeper, just as on a sandy beach!

Eastern edge of gypsum dunes, partially covered by shrubbery.
(National Park Service)

GEOLOGIC DIVISIONS

The Parks, Monuments, etc., as already noted, have been characterized by one or more of these geologic terms:

Batholithic
(Igneous Intrusive) — granitic mountain cores

Volcanic
(Igneous Extrusive) — volcanoes, lava flows

Sedimentation — strata of earth history

Diastrophism — folding and faulting movements

Erosion and
Deposition — wind and water action

Shorelines — ocean and lake action

Ground Water — caverns, swamps, geysers, springs

Glaciation — valley and continental glaciers

Mineralogy — mineral deposits, meteorites

Paleontology — fossil plants and animals

(Biology and Archeology — generally omitted)

Batholithic (Igneous Intrusive)

These masses formed from magmas which cooled deeply below the surface. Magmas are fluid bodies, mainly silicates of sodium, calcium, aluminum, iron, and magnesium, with steam among other gases. They rise because of their density being less than that for corresponding solids, and their ability to flux adjacent rocks into liquids. They must not be confused with the main liquefied mass or zone which is believed to exist nearer to the earth's core.

Intrusive masses may exist as many types: (a) batholiths — the largest of all, with no known floor, and hundreds of thousands of square miles in area; (b) laccoliths — the mushroom shaped bodies with level floors and domed tops, intruded between the strata; (c) dikes — sheets intruded across strata, varying in thickness and area; and (d) sills — tabular masses intruded between and parallel to the strata, likewise variable in size.

Granite is the most common rock in the first two largest masses. It is coarse-grained from slower cooling and crystallization, and white, light gray, or pink to red in color.

Intrusive granite outcrop typical of the Boulder batholith, a portion of the Rocky Mountains near Butte, Mont.   (From color slide by the writer)

Darker coarse-grained intrusives are designated by other names, based on mineral constituents. Basalt commonly forms the two smaller bodies named. It is a densely fine-grained, rather heavy rock, black, greenish-black, or weathered to a reddish-brown color. Likewise, there are other fine-grained rocks of lighter colors, formed of acidic silicates instead of basic ones.

Volcanic (Igneous Extrusive)

Volcanic lava flows may be expelled from vents in the flanks of a cone as well as from the central crater. Immense flows have also issued from fissures in the surface of the earth, far from any volcano. The exploded materials may also be blown for thousands of miles before deposition. Lava flows are mainly of porous basalt, or scoria, caused by gas bubbles. The material originates deep in the crust of the earth, liquifying because of pressures, radioactive processes, and so on.

Surface "malpais" flow of lava, mainly of the scoria or "aa" type. West of Carrizozo, N.M.　　　　(From color slide by the writer)

Diastrophism

Movements of the earth's crust are called diastrophism, and these may result in gigantic structural features, such as the huge Sierra Nevada fault scarp, or tiny fractures in a hand specimen. Many mountain valleys originate as faults, and the rocks themselves may have become compressed or recrystallized. Mineral reactions in such zones may often produce metallurgical mining areas, or scenic beauty may be the sole result of great significance.

Earthquakes are undoubtedly the most terrifying and tragic of earth phenomena - unless one lives at the foot of an active volcano!

The San Francisco earthquake of April 18, 1906 registered 8.25 on the Richter Scale of Intensity, which has a theoretical maximum of 10. Subsequent shocks along this San Andreas fault have continued into recent times, as well as in other California areas.

Earthquake debris which swept from the bare mountain slope at the left across the Madison River and far up the southward side. The boulder at the right bears a plaque stating names of the 19 persons buried beneath. (From color slide by the writer)

The writer experienced the Helena, Montana earthquake tremors between October 18 and 31, 1935, of which there were four major shocks followed by more than a thousand minor jolts for months afterward.

Near midnight on August 17, 1950, an earthquake shook the area near the Hebgen Reservoir in the Madison River valley not far from West Yellowstone. This caused a huge landslide which rode across the valley and up the far side, killing many campers and burying the bodies of 19 which were never recovered. Yellowstone Park geysers were somewhat affected.

The greatest earthquake ever to strike North America was that of Good Friday, March 27, 1964, at Anchorage, Alaska, which was officially recorded at 8.4 on the Richter scale. A graben or down-faulted block passed diagonally through the heart of the city, dropping the north side of its main street, 4th Avenue, primarily between C and D Streets, about 20 feet below its former level, and demolishing all buildings on that side, although those on the south side were comparatively undamaged. Loss of life might have been even greater earlier in the day.

North side of 4th Ave. between C and D Streets. Center of graben was at 4th and D. Anchorage, Alaska, Good Friday, March 27, 1964, 5:36 p.m. (Stewart's Photo Shop)

A great many expensive homes of the $50,000 — $100,000 type slid off the cliff at Turnagain Arm into Cook Inlet, likewise with loss of many lives.

The port city of Valdez on Resurrection Bay, south of Anchorage about 100 miles, was destroyed by a tidal wave which hurled itself against and over a wharf where many people were watching the unloading of a freighter.

The epicenter of this earthquake is believed to have been toward the east, near the town of Whittier, at a shallow depth.

Of course, earthquakes occur all over the world resulting in tremendous loss of property and life. The recent ones in Mexico and Chile exemplify such tragedies.

Earthquake Park, at Turnagain Arm site, Anchorage, Alaska, where many $50,000- $100,000 homes were demolished, sliding into Cook Inlet during the March 27, 1964 earthquake.

(From color slide by Mac's Foto Service)

Sedimentation

Earth processes are both constructive and destructive. The igneous granite of today may be weathered to the sedimentary sandstone of the geologic tomorrow, then later on compressed to the metamorphic quartzite of the geologic day after tomorrow.

In canyons, in cliffs, even in highway cuts, as well as while crossing folded strata, one can study the sequence of formations deposited during hundreds of millions of years. Or an uneven boundary between two such layers may indicate a gap in the record, known as an **unconformity**, caused when erosion was taking place.

Stratigraphic section exposed by Colorado River erosion. Precambrian metamorphics form the bottom of the gorge; Paleozoic sediments are predominant in the terraced walls of the main canyon; a remnant of Mesozoic sediment exists in the upper right portion of the photograph. Grand Canyon, Ariz.   (From color slide by the writer)

Erosion and Deposition

The entire surface of the land is subject to the unceasing ravages of wind, water, ice or atmosphere. Moreover, there are some areas where these agents of erosion are primarily responsible for the scenery which has prompted designation as a national park or a monument. Such localities are usually found where the rocks are younger and softer than elsewhere. In moist areas, streams erode valleys and canyons, carrying the material downstream to more level locations, where rivers become choked with sandbars, or to lakes and oceans, where the sediment is deposited as deltas.

Glaciated valleys are distinguished by their U-shaped profile, in contrast to the V-shape of river valleys. Glacial deposits have many forms, such as moraines, eskers, and drumlins.

Colorado River at low water stage within the Grand Canyon. The River Trail is barely visible at the left. View is westward, downstream.

(From color slide by the writer)

190

Shorelines

Shorelines of oceans and lakes may be features of much geologic interest, oceanic types being of most significance. In general, they are a direct result of transportation and accumulation of materials by winds, waves, or currents. Yet the nature of the bedrock and subsequent influences of earth history as faulting or glaciation will also be recognized.

Some very unique shoreline features are bars, spits, hooks, barrier reefs, also beaches and islands caused by deposition, with erosion producing wave-cut cliffs, sea caves, arches, stacks, and terraces.

Shoreline display of the Pacific Ocean taken from sea cliff showing sandy beach at low tide and eroded stacks.

Near Gold Beach, Ore. (From color slide by the writer)

Ground Water

Caverns are created when the surface waters, mildly acidified by carbon dioxide of the air and organic acids from decaying vegetation, contact massive limestone beds fractured by jointing. The insoluble calcium carbonate is converted to the soluble bicarbonate and carried away by the subsurface drainage leaving open spaces in the rock.

Sometimes the mineralized water will seep through the ceilings of associated caves at lower levels, evaporate, and leave calcium carbonate again as stalactites pendant from the ceilings, stalagmites accumulating on the floors, or helictites on the walls. Draperies, nodules, and other shapes are also well known.

Springs and geysers are also common evidences of ground water flow.

Layers of travertine deposited by ground water emerging as hot springs near Wind River, Thermopolis, Wyo. (From color slide by the writer)

Glaciation

Our world may still be considered as being in the final portion of the Pleistocene Glacial Epoch, since 10% of the present land surface is yet buried beneath ice, chiefly in Antarctica and Greenland. This major, best-known time of glaciation began about two million years ago. The ice sheets spread in all directions from centers in northern Canada, also in Eurasia, and advanced four times into the United States, covering New England and New York, the Great Lakes, and extending on about as far southward as the channels of the Ohio and Missouri Rivers, which developed along the ice front. Peaks at higher elevations, as in the Rocky Mountains, Cascades, and Coast Ranges had their own glacial pattern, as today. The last significant withdrawal of ice within the Northern Hemisphere occurred about 15,000 years ago.

Deposits of rocky debrism such as moraines, eskers, drumlins, outwash plains, etc. are well known, while glacial erosion may produce U-shaped valleys, hanging valleys, cirques, arretes, and other forms pictured in geology texts.

Air view of Knik Glacier, which forms an annual lake in the Knik River northeast of Anchorage, Alaska, until "calving" of its front results in a self-dumping action of water flooding into the Matanuska River.

(From color slide by the writer)

Glaciers are of three types: (1) continental ice sheets, mentioned above, of which those of Antarctica and Greenland are the remaining examples; (2) piedmont glaciers, formed by the junction of valley glaciers below the mountain slopes; and (3) valley or Alpine glaciers, the most common, as in such areas as Alaska, Glacier National Park, and lofty mountain ranges all over the world. They may vary greatly in size and rapidity of movement, which may produce an advancing, retreating, or stationary front depending on the ratio between ice accumulation above and melting below.

The writer's Geology class on a field trip to the frontal crevasses of Matanuska Glacier, 100 miles northeast of Anchorage, Alaska.

(From color slide by the writer)

There were previous times of glaciation as well, such as in the Precambrian and in the Permian, but no traces of these can be seen now by anyone but a geologist. Many of our present topographic features are either a direct result of glaciers or of erosion and deposition related to them. Latest engineering measurements of glacial movement in Alaska, Washington, Montana, and also in Europe indicate that while most of the glacial fronts are retreating, some do show times of advancement. The Glacial Epoch has not yet ended!

Mineralogy

Many minerals of course occur within national reserve areas, such as calcite formations in caves, quartz crystals in veins or geodes, jasper and agate in petrified wood, or lime and silica in hydrothermal regions. But the only national monuments which feature a mineral deposit as such are White Sands (gypsum) in New Mexico, and Pipestone (red catlinite) in Minnesota.

Craters formed by fallen meteorites, composed of native iron or iron-nickel alloys plus stony material would also come into this category, although none are included within the National Parks or Monuments.

Collection of meteorites from the Canyon Diablo area where the noted Barringer Meteor Crater is located. They are mostly of the iron-nickel type, although some are more stony in composition.

Meteor Crater, west of Winslow, Ariz.   (From color slide by the writer)

Paleontology

Fossils technically include remains or traces of pre-historic life, including the actual bodies frozen in permafrost areas of Siberia or Alaska, or preserved in the tar pits at La Brea, California, also bones, teeth, and shells of land or water-living creatures, mineralized wood, imprints of skin, bark, or even tracks. Sometimes the impressions of the body form a mold, which later may be filled with mineral matter to create a replica, or cast.

The Petrified Forest of Arizona, the Dinosaur National Monument of Utah-Colorado, in addition to the recently added Florissant Fossil Beds National Monument in Colorado emphasize this field of study.

The Silurian trilobite, *Dalmanites limulurus*, shown in about its natural size. These creatures, belonging to the highest invertebrate group, appeared suddenly in Cambrian paleontology, and dominated the seas for many hundreds of millions of years before becoming extinct at the end of the Paleozoic era.   (From color slide from Ward's Nat. Sci. Est.)

Three general groups of rocks, based upon their mode of origin, are universally recognized:

1. IGNEOUS rocks, which were formed as a direct result of cooling and crystallization of molten material. These are broadly subdivided into two major types:

a) **Intrusive**, which were cooled below the earth's surface very slowly, thus producing large crystals. Granite is the best known example of these coarsely crystalline forms, often in cores of major mountain ranges. Diorite is also coarsely crystalline, but darker because of more iron minerals.

b) **Extrusive**, which were cooled more rapidly near or upon the surface. Rhyolite is the finely crystalline equivalent of Granite and Obsidian is the glassy extrusive chemical equivalent in many surface flows. Basalt is the darker dense type, usually known as Scoria or Lava when it is extremely porous. Pumice is more finely porous, so very light from interior air spaces that it will float upon water. It forms as a result of violent volcanic explosions.

Non-crystalline fragmental forms, also of explosive origin, are Tuff — irregular small pieces — and Ash — dustlike particles. Both of these may be carried by atmospheric currents over wide areas.

2. SEDIMENTARY rocks, which were formed as deposits of material by wind, water, or ice, usually show some stratification. They often are subdivided into (a) mechanical, (b) organic, and (c) chemical groups. Conglomerate is composed of rounded gravel or pebbles, cemented together with lime or silica. Breccia is similarly composed of cemented angular fragments. Sandstone is obviously formed of sand granules, often with a red iron oxide cementing material, especially common in the Southwest. Shale is a product of mud or clay. Limestone usually has been derived from organic shell fragments, with or without visible fossils, but may also be a result of chemical precipitation.

3. METAMORPHIC rocks, produced by effects of heat and/or pressure of mountain-building forces, may originate from former igneous or sedimentary rocks. For example, a Granite may be transformed into a banded Gneiss, although other origins are also possible. Many finely-crystalline rocks may become a Schist. Sandstone may harden and recrystallize into Quartzite, a sandy shale into Argillite, a pure Shale into Slate, or a Limestone into Marble.

197

IGNEOUS ROCKS

Granite — coarsely crystalline, containing mainly quartz, feldspar, and hornblende.
Along Columbia River near Wenatchee, Wash., transported from the Cascade Range.

Diorite — coarsely crystalline, containing about 50% feldspar and hornblende.
Pecos Wilderness, N.M.

Rhyolite — finely crystalline, granitic composition, showing layers from sill flowage.
Corkscrew Canyon, Socorro, N.M.

Pumice — extremely porous type formed by explosive eruption.
Lake bed east of Crater Lake, Ore.

Obsidian — glassy texture, black (or reddish) due to rapid surface flowage and cooling.
South of Bend, Ore.

Obsidian — layers intermingled with sediments, from surface flowage. Jemez Mountains, New Mexico.

Basalt — finely crystalline, same constituents as more coarsely crystalline dark igneous rock.
Mount Lassen, Cal.

Basalt, Columnar — finely crystalline, constituents as above, with hexagonal joints from contractual cooling.
Near Crystal, N.M.

Basalt (Scoria or Lava) — "aa" or vesicular type formed by gaseous bubbles.
Mount Shasta, Cal.

Basalt (Scoria or Lava) — "pahoehoe" or ropy type formed by flow cooling.
Carrizozo, N.M.

Conglomerate — rounded pebbles or gravel cemented together by silica or lime.
Near Silver City, N.M.

Breccia — angular fragments cemented together by silica, lime, or as here, by a reddish form of silica called jasper.
Southern Black Hills, So. Dak.

Sandstone — sand grains cemented together by silica or lime, which may be stratified as shown here, or massive.
Near Gallup, N.M.

Sandstone —micro-faulted, showing on a small scale similar major faults which may occur in the earth's crust, causing earthquakes.
Calico Canyon, southern Black Hills, So. Dak.

Sandstone, red from contained iron oxide — showing cross-bedding caused by shallow-water currents. (Wind may also cause cross-bedding as in sand dunes.)
Near Holbrook, Ariz.

Sandstone, Fossiliferous — sand grains, as above, containing clam shells.
Near Gallup, N.M.

Shale, Carbonaceous — mud or clay material, here adjacent to coal strata.
Near Gallup, N.M.

Limestone, Creamy, Fine grained — lime or calcium carbonate, possibly organic.
Core formation of Arbuckle Mts., Okla.

Limestone, Gray, Crystalline -- lime or calcium carbonate, probably compressed organic fragments.
Rocky Mts., Mont.

Limestone, Fossiliferous — marine lime formation, containing brachiopods (a bivalve).
Zuni Mts., south of Gallup, N.M.

Limestone, Fossiliferous — marine lime formation, containing bryo-zoans ("moss animals").
Near Carlin, Nev.

Limestone, Fossiliferous — marine lime formation, containing crinoid ("sea-lily") stem fragments.
South-central Tex.

METAMORPHIC ROCKS

Gneiss — formed usually from Granite, but compressed and folded into layers of constituent minerals.
Bottom of Colorado R. gorge, Grand Canyon, Ariz.

Gneissoid-Schist — formed from some fine material, compressed and extremely folded.
Near Anchorage, Alaska

Schist, Micaceous — greatly foliated and crumpled through pressure and heat.
Central Colo. (Specimen from Ward's Nat. Sci. Est.)

Schist, Garnetiferous — this garnet crystal, and smaller ones contained in the specimen, was formed through chemical recrystallization under pressure and heat.
Wrangell, Alaska

Argillite — typically formed in western states from a sandy Shale, greatly compressed and jointed during pressure and heat.
Near West Glacier, Mont.

Argillite — as above, but here a typical shore line deposit showing mud cracks from drying, later to be re-filled with sediment.
Near West Glacier, Mont.

Slate, Black -- fine-grained former carbonaceous Shale, here showing original stratification as vertical banding, plus subsequent joint-planes from pressure.

Near Bangor, Penn. (Specimen from Ward's Nat. Sci. Est.)

Marble, White, Crystalline — originally a pure limestone, now compressed and recrystallized.

Near West Rutland, Vt. (Specimen from Ward's Nat. Sci. Est.)

Quartzite — originally a cross-bedded Sandstone, now greatly compressed and recrystallized.
Near El Paso, Tex.

Quartzitic Conglomerate — Quartz pebbles recrystallized and surficially worn by stream action.
Near Farmington, N.M.

REFERENCE SOURCES

GENERAL PARK AND MONUMENT BOOKS
(Arranged for reader convenience
by title, rather than by author.)

America's National Parks — Kodak Guide. Frome, Michael — Eastman Kodak Co. New York: Popular Library, 1969.

America's Wonderlands — The Scenic National Parks and Monuments of the United States. Washington, D.C.: National Geographic Society, 1959.

Exploring Our National Parks and Monuments. Butcher, Devereaux. (6th ed./rev.) Boston: Houghton, Mifflin Co., 1969.

Guide to the National Parks, A: Their Landscape and Geology. (2 vol.) Matthews, William H. III. Garden City, N.Y.: The Natural History Press, 1968.

National Parks of the West. Sunset Books and Sunset Magazine. Menlo Park, Cal.: Lane Magazine and Book Co., 1965.

National Parks, The. Tilden, Freeman. New York: Alfred A. Knopf 1968.

Our Country's National Parks. (2 vol.) Melbo, Irving H. Indianapolis: Bobbs-Merrill, 1941.

Our National Parks in Color. Butcher, Devereaux. New York: Clarkson N. Potter, 1969.

Parks for America. U.S. National Park Service. Washington, D.C.: Department of the Interior, 1964.

(and others)

SPECIFIC PARK AND MONUMENT BROCHURES
(Arranged for reader convenience alphabetically by states, rather than by author.)

ARIZONA
Grand Canyon — The Story Behind the Scenery. Beal, Merrill D. Flagstaff, Ariz.: KC Publications, 1967.

Meteor Crater Story, The. Foster, George. Winslow, Ariz.: Meteor Crater Enterprises, Inc., 1964.

Petrified Forest — The Story Behind the Scenery. Ash, Sidney R. and David D. May. Holbrook, Ariz.: Petrified Forest Museum Asso., 1969.

CALIFORNIA
Rancho La Brea — A Record of Pleistocene Life in California. (Not NPS) Stock, Chester. Los Angeles: Los Angeles County Museum, 1965.

Geology of Lassen's Landscape. Schulz, Paul E. Mineral, Cal.: Loomis Museum Asso., Lassen Volcanic National Park, 1959.

Natural History of the Pinnacles National Monument. Bennett, Peter S. San Benito County, Cal.: Pinnacles Natural History Asso., 1969.

Sequoia and Kings Canyon National Parks. White, John R. and Samuel J. Pusateri. Stanford, Cal.: Stanford University Press, 1949.

Yosemite Story, The. Huntington, Harriet E. Garden City, N.Y.: Doubleday & Co., 1966.

HAWAII
Volcanoes of the National Parks in Hawaii. MacDonald, Gordon A. and Douglass H. Hubbard, Hawaii Natural History Asso., 1961.

MONTANA
Geologic Story of Glacier National Park, The. Dyson, James L. West Glacier, Mont.: Glacier Natural History Asso., 1960.

Glaciers and Glaciation in Glacier National Park. Dyson, James L. West Glacier, Mont.: Glacier Natural History Asso., 1966.

NEW MEXICO

America's Scenic Wonderland – Carlsbad Caverns National Park. Barnett, John. Fresno, Cal.: Awani Press, 1969.

Guide Book to Carlsbad Caverns National Park. Editor: Paul F. Spangle. Guide Book Series No. 1. Washington, D.C.: The National Speleological Society, 1960.

OREGON

Underworld of Oregon Caves. Contor, Roger J. Klamath Falls, Ore.: Crater Lake Natural History Asso., 1963.

UTAH, ARIZONA, NEW MEXICO, etc.

Your National Park System in the Southwest. Jackson, Earl. Globe, Ariz.: Southwestern Monuments Asso., and Phoenix, Ariz.: McGrew Printing & Lithographing Co., 1967.

UTAH, COLORADO, WYOMING

Geologic Story of the Uinta Mountains, The. Hansen, Wallace R. Washington, D.C.: Geological Survey, Department of the Interior, 1969.

UTAH, ARIZONA

Ancient Landscapes of the Grand Canyon Region. McFee, Eswin D. Flagstaff, Ariz.: Sun Printers, 1958.

UTAH

Desert Solitaire – A Season in the Wilderness. Abbey, Edward. New York: Ballentine Books, Inc., 1971.

Grater's Guide to Zion, Bryce Canyon, Cedar Breaks. Grater, Russell K. Portland, Ore.: Binfords & Mort, 1950.

Dinosaur Quarry, The. Good, John M., Theodore E. White, and Gilbert F. Stucker. Washington, D.C.: National Park Service, Department of the Interior, 1958.

World of the Dinosaurs, The. Dunkle, David H. Washington, D.C.: Smithsonian Institution, 1966.

WASHINGTON

Geologic Story of Mount Rainier, The. Crandell, Dwight R. Washington, D.C.: Geological Survey Bulletin 1292, 1969.

Grater's Guide to Mount Rainier National Park. Grater, Russell K. Portland, Ore.: Binfords & Mort, 1949.

WYOMING

Creation of the Teton Landscape. Love, J.D. and John C. Reed, Jr. Washington, D.C.: Geological Survey, Department of the Interior, 1968.

Washburn Yellowstone Expedition, The. from The Overland Monthly, Vol. 6 — May, June, 1871 — Nos. 5, 6. Facsimile Reproduction. Seattle, Wash.: The Shorey Book Store, 1964.

Geologic Story of Yellowstone National Park, The. Keefer, William R. Washington, D.C.: Geological Survey 1347, 1972.

Many other similar brochures or pamphlets can be obtained free or at low cost at individual National Park offices, or from the National Park Service, Washington, D.C. 20240.

GEOLOGY TEXTBOOKS
(Arranged alphabetically by author.)

Baldwin, Ewart M. *Geology of Oregon.* Ann Arbor, Mich.: Edwards Brothers, Inc., 1964.

Dunbar, Carl O. and Karl M. Waage. *Historical Geology.* (3rd ed.) New York: John Wiley & Sons, 1969.

Ekman, Leonard C. *Scenic Geology of the Pacific Northwest.* (2nd ed.) Portland, Ore.: Binfords & Mort, 1962.

Emmons, William H., et al. *Geology: Principles and Processes.* New York: McGraw-Hill Book Co., 1960.

Gilluly, James, A.C. Waters, and A.O. Woodford. *Principles of Geology.* (2nd ed.) San Francisco: W.H. Freeman & Co., 1959.

Leet, L. Don and Sheldon Judson. *Physical Geology.* (4th ed.) Englewood Cliffs, N.J.: Prentice-Hall, 1971.

Longwell, Chester R., Adolph Knopf, and Richard F. Flint. *Physical Geology.* (3rd ed.) New York: John Wiley & Sons, 1953.

Moore, Raymond C. *Introduction to Historical Geology.* (2nd ed.) New York: McGraw-Hill Book Co., 1958.

Putnam, William C. *Geology.* New York: Oxford University Press, 1964.

Shelton, John S. *Geology Illustrated.* San Francisco: 1966.

Wyckoff, Jerome. *Rock, Time, and Landforms.* New York: Harper & Row, 1966.

(and many others)

ACKNOWLEDGMENTS

Early correspondence with officials of the National Park Service in Washington, D.C. included many comments and suggestions from Robert H. Rose, Chief Park Geologist (now retired), John R. Vosburgh, Chief in Branch of Features and Fred R. Bell, Visual Information Specialist, as well as his assistant, Clarence Kyle, who selected many prints for loaned use, even before the usual publishing agreement had been reached. Reduced photographic negatives of these were made by the writer.

The majority of photographs herein are duly credited to the National Park Service, under the Department of the Interior. Others were originally black-and-white photographs by the writer, or are black-and-white copies of some of his color slides, taken during many enjoyable trips through the National Parks of the western states. A few others are credited to various personal or commercial sources, used by their kind permission.

All pages of the manuscript were sent to offices of each National Park or Monument, requesting criticisms or suggestions. Practically every official replied promptly and cooperatively, such information being included in this final revision of several years intermittent writing.

All rock specimens photographed by the writer for this booklet were collected during many years from various localities (except as otherwise noted), and have recently been used in Community College classes in Geology in Alaska, New Mexico, and Oregon.

Thanks are also due to Dot Dotson's Photofinishing of Eugene, Oregon, who were especially cooperative in producing prints or enlargements of desired contrast, also in making black-and-white negatives from color slides, or for the two full page diagrams.

Copy was typeset by the Pluid Printing Parlour and by J. G. Graphics, Inc., both of Eugene, Oregon.

DESCRIPTION OF COVER PICTURES

MUIR GLACIER
St. Elias Range to E.,
Fairweather Range to W.
Glacier Bay N.M., Alaska
Schallerer's Photo Shop
Anchorage, Alaska

CRATER LAKE AND WIZARD ISLAND
Mt. Scott in background
Average diameter - 5 miles
Maximum depth - 1932 feet
Crater Lake N.P., Oregon
R. C. Rowe

MT. GRINNELL, GRINNELL GLACIER, LAKE SHERBURNE
E. of Continental Divide
Glacier N.P., Montana
R. C. Rowe

YOSEMITE FALLS
Upper Fall   - 1430 feet
Middle Cascades -   675 feet
Lower Fall   -   320 feet
Total drop   - 2425 feet
(Second highest in world)
Yosemite N.P., California
Ward's Natural Science Est.
Rochester, N.Y.

LAVA FOUNTAIN, KILAUEA IKI
1959 eruption, 1500 feet high
Hawaii Volcanoes N.P., Hawaii
Ward's Natural Science Est.
Rochester, New York

RAINBOW BRIDGE
309 feet high, 278 foot span
33-42 feet wide - largest in
the world
Rainbow Bridge N.M., Utah
John Keist, Continental Divide, New Mexico